Programming and Deploying
Java™ Mobile Agents
with Aglets™

Programming and Deploying Java™ Mobile Agents with Aglets™

Danny B. Lange
Mitsuru Oshima

ADDISON-WESLEY

An imprint of Addison Wesley Longman, Inc.

Reading, Massachusetts • Harlow, England • Menlo Park, California
Berkeley, California • Don Mills, Ontario • Sydney
Bonn • Amsterdam • Tokyo • Mexico City

The publisher offers discounts on this book when ordered in quantity for special sales. For more information, please contact:

Corporate, Government, and Special Sales Group
Addison Wesley Longman, Inc.
One Jacob Way
Reading, Massachusetts 01867

Library of Congress Cataloging-in-Publication Data

Lange, Danny B.
    Programming and deploying Java mobile agents with aglets / Danny B.
Lange, Mitsuru Oshima.
        p.   cm.
    Includes bibliographical references and index.
    ISBN 0-201-32582-9 (alk. paper)
    1. Mobile agents (Computer software)   2. Java (Computer program
language)   I. Oshima, Mitsuru.   II. Title.
QA76.76.I58L36   1998
005.2'762--dc21   98-20525
                                                                CIP

ISBN 0-201-32582-9

Text printed on recycled and acid-free paper.

1 2 3 4 5 6 7 8 9 10 – MA – 02 01 00 99 98
First printing, August 1998

To Eva, Jacob, and Yina
Danny B. Lange

To Akiko and Yuka
Mitsuru Oshima

Contents

Preface

Think of the Internet as a distributed, massively parallel supercomputer that connects information repositories, databases, intelligent agents, and mobile code. Imagine sending your own personalized agents to roam the Internet. They will monitor your favorite Web sites, get you the ticket you couldn't get at the box office, or help you to remotely schedule meetings for your next overseas trip. Sound like science fiction? Maybe, but the advent of Java has truly revolutionized the Internet. It has created a global infrastructure that is just waiting for mobile agents to roam its wires and interact with millions of computers.

Who Should Read This Book?

This book is about how to program mobile Internet agents in Java with the help of the Aglet application programming interface (API). A freely available implementation of the Aglet API from IBM Corporation has spurred a tremendous interest in aglets. Consequently, there have been numerous calls for a reference book on the aglet, its API, and its use.

As the inventors of the aglet, we decided to put in some long nights to write the definitive book about how to program Java aglets. We hope you enjoy reading it. The book is intended for daring programmers, students, and researchers at the frontier of network programming. No particular knowledge about agent-related technologies is required, but fluency in Java is a must.

Organization of This Book

The following outline shows the progression of the material we present. Chapters 1 and 2 are a general introduction to various aspects of the mobile agent paradigm. Chapter 3 provides a bridge between the mobile agent paradigm and Java by introducing the Aglet API. Chapters 4 through 7 systematically cover the Aglet API in detail, and Chapters 8 through 10 are dedicated to advanced subjects: agent design patterns, the Aglet API and its implementation, and mobile agent security.

Chapter 1: Introduction to Mobile Agents

This chapter leads you into the world of mobile agents, an emerging technology that makes it much easier to design, implement, and maintain distributed systems. We explain the benefits of mobile agents and demonstrate their impact on the design of distributed systems. The chapter also includes a brief overview of contemporary mobile agent systems.

Chapter 2: Elements of a Mobile Agent System

This chapter helps you to develop a basic understanding of the elements of a mobile agent system. We present the basic conceptual model of mobile agents, which includes the two core concepts of any mobile agent system: agent and place. The chapter also describes the essentials of agent behavior, including the creation and disposal of agents and their transfer over a network.

Chapter 3: Mobile Agents with Java

This chapter shows what it is that makes Java a powerful tool for agent development. This chapter introduces you to the aglet—a Java-based agile agent—and gives you a brief overview of the Aglet API. The purpose of this overview is to link the mobile agent model with Java.

Chapter 4: Anatomy of an Aglet

This chapter teaches you about the methods in the `Aglet` class that can be overridden by the programmer. These methods are systematically invoked by the system as important events in the life of an aglet. The chapter shows you the principles of using these methods, including important information about the order in which they are invoked by the system when specific events take place. With this knowledge, you will be in a position to create aglets that can perform simple tasks on remote computers.

Chapter 5: Aglet Context

This chapter covers one of the key elements of the Aglet API, namely, the `Aglet-Context` interface. The interface defines the execution context for aglets, and in this chapter we teach you about the methods that an aglet can invoke in its current context to create new aglets, retrieve aglets contained in the same as well as remote contexts, and much more.

Chapter 6: Aglet Messaging

This chapter covers the basics of aglet messaging. Several means of interaglet communication are supported in the Aglet API, and you will learn about simple messaging with and without reply, advanced message management, and multicast messaging between aglets. The classes covered in this chapter include `Message`, `MessageManager`, and `FutureReply`.

Chapter 7: Aglet Collaboration

This chapter introduces the aglet proxy, `AgletProxy`, and describes the rationale behind this important element of the Aglet API. This overview is followed by a demonstration of different ways to control aglets to make them collaborate with one another.

Chapter 8: Agent Design Patterns

This chapter focuses on a set of design patterns for creating mobile agent applications. Design patterns have proved to be highly useful in object-oriented programming and have helped developers to achieve good design of applications through reusability of validated components. We hope that the design patterns described in this chapter will serve this purpose in the context of aglet-based applications.

Chapter 9: Inside Aglets

This chapter presents a general overview of the components of the Aglets framework, with a special focus on selected parts of the framework. After reading this chapter you should have a sufficient understanding of the inner workings of the Aglets Framework to optimize the performance of your aglets, to understand why apparently healthy aglets are malfunctioning, and overall to better use the Aglet API in your programming.

Chapter 10: Aglet Security

This chapter introduces you to network security technologies in general and mobile agent security in particular. We first show you what can go wrong when mobile agents are released in a network. This is followed by a taxonomy of attacks, which introduces you to some potential attacks related to mobile agents. We then briefly explain cryptography as a general basis of security before continuing with a description of the set of security services available for mobile agents. The remainder of this chapter is devoted to a description of security policies for mobile agent systems in general and the Aglets framework in particular.

Appendix: The Aglet API Documentation

The appendix contains the API documentation of the Aglet API (limited to the `aglet` package).

Bibliography

We offer this list of works for further reading on related topics. The list is by no means exhaustive, and other excellent works exist on most of the topics.

Conventions Used in This Book

All the code examples in the text have been compiled and run on Java Development Kit (JDK) 1.1.5 using the first release of IBM's Aglets Software Development Kit. Source code for examples in this book can be retrieved on-line from the Web sites listed in the Introduction.

A constant-width font is used for the following:

- Code examples

```
public class MyFirstAglet extends Aglet {
    ...
}
```

- Class, method, and variable names within the text
- URLs set in italics

We have attempted to be complete and accurate throughout this book. Changes in future releases of IBM's Aglets Software Development Kit, as well as changes in future releases of JavaSoft's JDK, make it impossible to be completely accurate in all cases. We welcome your feedback about this book, especially if you spot errors or omissions. We prefer to use the Aglets mailing list (see the Introduction) as the communication channel for this book. However, if you wish to contact us directly, feel free to send your electronic mail to *danny@acm.org*.

Additional information as well as example source code, updates, and corrections to this book can be found at the publisher's Web site: `http://www.awl.com/cseng/titles/0-201-32582-9`.

Acknowledgments

As you are probably well aware, writing a book is never an effort undertaken solely by the authors who get all the credit on the cover. Many people have contributed, helped, and encouraged us in a great many ways.

First, our thanks go to the past and present members of the Aglets Team at IBM, without whom aglets would not have made it. They include, in alphabetical order, Dr. Yariv Aridor, Gunter Karjoth, Kazuya Kosaka, Yoshiaki Mima, Dr. Yuichi Nakamura, Kouichi Ono, Hideaki Tai, Kazuyuki Tsuda, and Gaku Yamamoto. Special thanks to Dr. Tsutomu Kamimura; without his unflagging support, aglets would not have seen the light of day. We would also like to thank Mike McDonald of IBM Japan for checking the wording of this book.

Many people at Addison-Wesley contributed to our project. In particular we wish to thank Betsy Hardinger, Katherine Kwack, Mary O'Brien, Laura Potter, Marilyn Rash, and Elizabeth Spainhour for their editorial and production support. We would also like to thank all the reviewers for their insights and valuable comments at various stages of the creation of this book: Michael Bursell, Paul Clements, Ross A. Finlayson, James P. Neill, and Alan Piszcz.

Most of all, we must thank our respective families. Mitsuru thanks Akiko for her tolerant support and little Yuka for slumbering peacefully during the writing of this book. Danny wishes to thank Eva, Jacob, and Yina for their tireless support and for being never-failing sources of wonderful diversion during the work of making aglets a reality and later during the writing of this book.

Have a good time with aglets!

Danny B. Lange   Mitsuru Oshima
Cupertino, California   *Tokyo, Japan*

Introduction

Why All the Fuss about Mobile Agents?

Software *agents* are programs that assist people and act on their behalf. Agents function by allowing people to delegate work to them. This is a very interesting concept that becomes even more attractive when the agents are no longer bound to the system where they begin execution.

Mobile agents have the unique ability to transport themselves from one system in a network to another. The ability to travel allows mobile agents to move to a system that contains services with which they want to interact and then to take advantage of being in the same host or network as the service (see Figure I-1).

You will find that mobile agents reduce network traffic and provide an effective means of overcoming network latency. What's more, through their ability to operate asynchronously and independently of the process that created them, mobile agents help you to construct highly robust and fault-tolerant systems.

Several organizations promote standards for mobile agent systems. Two of them are the Object Management Group (OMG) and the Foundation for Intelligent and Physical Agents (FIPA). Together they represent almost 1,000 corporate members. OMG endorses the Mobile Agent System Interoperability Facility (MASIF); at the time of this writing, FIPA has called for proposals for agent

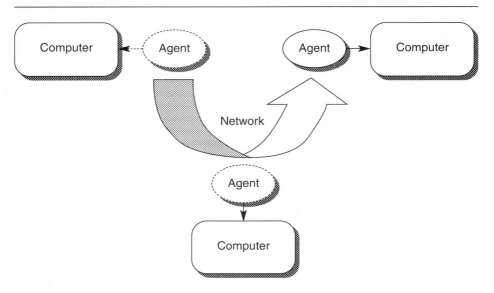

FIGURE I-1   Mobile Agent Traveling from Computer to Computer

mobility. We expect these standardization efforts to have a positive effect on the deployment of mobile agents in commercial systems.

What Is a Java Aglet?

The *aglet* represents the next leap forward in the evolution of executable content on the Internet, introducing program code that can be transported along with state information. Aglets are Java objects that can move from one host on the Internet to another. That is, an aglet that executes on one host can suddenly halt execution, dispatch itself to a remote host, and resume execution there. When the aglet moves, it takes along its program code as well as its data.

The aglet is a mobile Java agent that supports the concepts of autonomous execution and dynamic routing on its itinerary. You can also think of the aglet as a generalization and extension of Java applets and servlets. Aglets are hosted by an Aglet server in a way similar to the way applets are hosted by a Web browser (see Figure I-2). The Aglet server provides an environment for aglets to execute in, and the Java virtual machine (JVM) and the Aglet security manager make it safe to receive and host aglets.

By the way, the origin of the word *aglet* is simple: it means "lightweight agent" in much the same way that *applet* means lightweight application. The term *aglet* is a portmanteau word combining *agent* and *applet*.

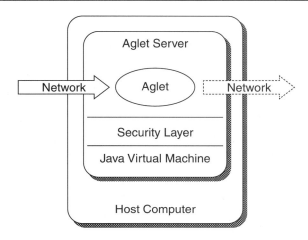

FIGURE I-2   Safe Hosting of Incoming Aglet

What Is the Aglet API?

The Aglet API is an agent development kit—in other words, a set of Java classes and interfaces that allows you to create mobile Java agents. A research team at the IBM Tokyo Research Laboratory developed the Aglet API in Japan in response to a call for a uniform platform for mobile agents in heterogeneous environments such as the Internet. The effort was initiated by one of the authors of this book, Danny B. Lange, in early 1995 and continues under the leadership of Mitsuru Oshima.

What is new about the Aglet API is that it stretches the renowned "write once, run anywhere" capability of Java programs to apply to mobile agents. We would rephrase it to "write once, go anywhere." That is, once you have written an aglet, it will run on every machine that supports the Aglet API. You need not be concerned with the underlying hardware or operating system or with the nature of the particular implementation of the Aglet API on the host where your aglet is running. The Aglet API mirrors the applet model in Java. The goal has been to bring the flavor of mobility to the applet. We have attempted to make the Aglets' Framework an exercise in clean design, and it is our hope that applet programmers will appreciate the many ways in which the aglet model reflects the applet model.

IBM's Aglets Software Development Kit

The Aglets Software Development Kit (ASDK) is an implementation of the Aglet API that can be downloaded from IBM Tokyo Research Laboratory's Web site

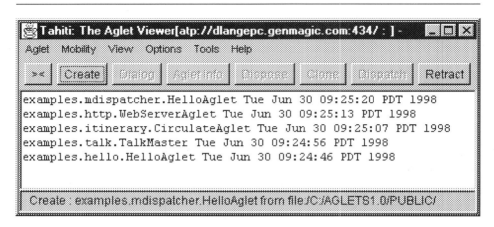

FIGURE I-3   A Screen Dump of the Tahiti Aglet Server

(*www.trl.ibm.co.jp/aglets*). The ASDK includes Aglet API packages, documentation, sample aglets, and the Tahiti aglet server (named after Danny's favorite vacation spot). Tahiti is a Java application that allows the user to receive, manage, and send aglets to other computers that are running Tahiti (see Figure I-3). You should use Tahiti to run the examples presented in this book.

World Wide Web and Mailing Lists

IBM's Aglets Web site can be found at *www.trl.ibm.co.jp/aglets*. Here you can find the latest releases and documentation of IBM's ASDK. Another important source of information is the Aglets mailing list, *aglets@javalounge.com*. Send a message with subscribe aglets in the message body to *aglets-request@javalounge.com*. If you wish to reach the Aglets Team, you should use *aglets@yamato.ibm.co.jp*.

Another interesting forum is the Mobility mailing list, *mobility@media.mit.edu*. Cofounded by Danny, this mailing list is dedicated to the discussion of mobile agent technology and applications. The last mailing list we want to mention is the much broader Agents mailing list, *agents@cs.umbc.edu*.

Chapter 1

Introduction to Mobile Agents

This chapter will lead you into the world of mobile agents, an emerging technology that makes it much easier to design, implement, and maintain distributed systems. You will find that mobile agents reduce network traffic and provide an effective means of overcoming network latency. Perhaps most important, through their ability to operate asynchronously and independently of the process that created them, they help you to construct highly robust and fault-tolerant systems, thereby directly or indirectly benefiting the end user.

Read on and let us introduce you to software agents, including mobile as well as stationary agents. We will explain the benefits of mobile agents and demonstrate the impact they have on the design of distributed systems. This chapter then concludes with a brief overview of some contemporary mobile agent systems.

1.1 What's a Software Agent?

The question of what actually constitutes an agent, and how it differs from other programs, has been heavily debated for several years. Although this debate is by no means over, we often see agents loosely defined as programs that assist people and act on their behalf. This is what we prefer to call the end-user perspective of software agents.

Agent (End-User Perspective)
An agent is a program that assists people and acts on their behalf. Agents function by allowing people to delegate work to them.

Although this definition is basically correct, it does not really get under the hood. Agents come in myriad different types and operate in many settings. They can be found in computer operating systems, networks, databases, and so on. What properties do these agents share that constitute the essence of being an agent?

This is not the place to examine the characteristics of the numerous agent systems made available to the public by many research labs. But if you looked at all these systems, you would find a property shared by all agents: the fact that they live in an environment. They have the ability to interact with their execution environment and to act asynchronously and autonomously upon it. No one is required either to deliver information to the agent or to consume any of its output. The agent simply acts continuously in pursuit of its own goals.

In contrast to the software objects of object-oriented programming, agents are active entities that work according to the so-called Hollywood principle: "Don't call us, we'll call you!"

Agent (System Perspective)
An agent is a software object that

- Is situated within an execution environment
- Possesses the following mandatory properties:
  - Reactive: senses changes in the environment and acts according to those changes
  - Autonomous: has control over its own actions
  - Goal-driven: is proactive
  - Temporally continuous: is continuously executing
- And may possess any of the following orthogonal properties:
  - Communicative: able to communicate with other agents
  - Mobile: can travel from one host to another
  - Learning: adapts in accordance with previous experience
  - Believable: appears believable to the end user

1.2   What's a Mobile Agent?

Mobility is an orthogonal property of agents—that is, not all agents are mobile. An agent can just sit there and communicate with its surroundings by conventional means, such as various forms of remote procedure calling and messaging. We call agents that do not or cannot move *stationary agents*.

Stationary Agent
A stationary agent executes only on the system where it begins execution. If it needs information that is not on that system or needs to interact with an agent

on a different system, it typically uses a communication mechanism such as remote procedure calling (RPC).

In contrast, a *mobile* agent is not bound to the system where it begins execution.
The mobile agent is free to travel among the hosts in the network. Created in one
execution environment, it can transport its state and code with it to another execution environment in the network, where it resumes execution.

By the term *state*, we typically mean the attribute values of the agent that
help it determine what to do when it resumes execution at its destination. By the
term *code*, we mean, in an object-oriented context, the class code necessary for the
agent to execute.

Mobile Agent

A mobile agent is not bound to the system where it begins execution. It has the
unique ability to transport itself from one system in a network to another. The
ability to travel allows a mobile agent to move to a system that contains an object
with which the agent wants to interact and then to take advantage of being in
the same host or network as the object.

1.3   Seven Good Reasons for Using Mobile Agents

Although mobile agent technology sounds exciting, our interest in mobile agents
should not be motivated by the technology per se but rather by the benefits
agents provide for the creation of distributed systems. Here are seven good reasons for you to start using mobile agents.

1. *They reduce the network load.* Distributed systems often rely on communications protocols that involve multiple interactions to accomplish a given task. This
is especially true when security measures are enabled. The result is a lot of network traffic. Mobile agents allow you to package a conversation and dispatch it
to a destination host, where the interactions can take place locally (see Figure 1-1).
Mobile agents are also useful when it comes to reducing the flow of raw data in
the network. When very large volumes of data are stored at remote hosts, these
data should be processed in the locality of the data rather than transferred over
the network. The motto is simple: move the computations to the data rather than
the data to the computations.

2. *They overcome network latency.* Critical real-time systems, such as robots in
manufacturing processes, need to respond in real time to changes in their environments. Controlling such systems through a factory network of a substantial size
involves significant latencies. For critical real-time systems, such latencies are not
acceptable. Mobile agents offer a solution, because they can be dispatched from a
central controller to act locally and directly execute the controller's directions.

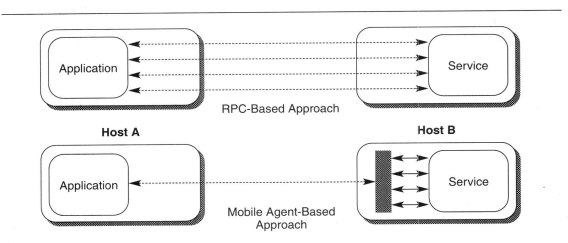

FIGURE 1-1   Mobile Agents and Network Load Reduction

3. *They encapsulate protocols.* When data are exchanged in a distributed system, each host owns the code that implements the protocols needed to properly code outgoing data and interpret incoming data, respectively. However, as protocols evolve to accommodate new requirements for efficiency or security, it is a cumbersome if not impossible task to upgrade protocol code properly. As a result, protocols often become a legacy problem. Mobile agents, on the other hand, can move to remote hosts to establish "channels" based on proprietary protocols.

4. *They execute asynchronously and autonomously.* Often, mobile devices must rely on expensive or fragile network connections. Tasks that require a continuously open connection between a mobile device and a fixed network probably will not be economically or technically feasible. To solve this problem, tasks can be embedded into mobile agents, which can then be dispatched into the network. After being dispatched, the mobile agents become independent of the creating process and can operate asynchronously and autonomously (see Figure 1-2). The mobile device can reconnect at a later time to collect the agent.

5. *They adapt dynamically.* Mobile agents have the ability to sense their execution environment and react autonomously to changes. Multiple mobile agents possess the unique ability to distribute themselves among the hosts in the network so as to maintain the optimal configuration for solving a particular problem.

6. *They are naturally heterogeneous.* Network computing is fundamentally heterogeneous, often from both a hardware and a software perspective. Because mobile agents are generally computer- and transport-layer-independent and are

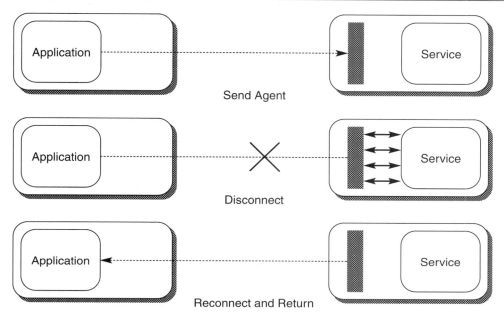

FIGURE 1-2   Mobile Agents and Disconnected Operation

dependent only on their execution environment, they provide optimal conditions for seamless system integration.

7. *They are robust and fault-tolerant.* The ability of mobile agents to react dynamically to unfavorable situations and events makes it easier to build robust and fault-tolerant distributed systems. If a host is being shut down, all agents executing on that machine will be warned and given time to dispatch and continue their operation on another host in the network.

1.4   Network Computing Paradigms

Our experience shows us that mobile agents provide a powerful, uniform paradigm for network computing. Mobile agents can revolutionize the design and development of distributed systems. To put this claim into perspective, we will provide a brief overview and comparison of three programming paradigms for distributed computing: client-server, code-on-demand, and mobile agents. Note that we put more emphasis on how the paradigm is perceived by the developer than on the underlying hardware-software architecture.

1.4.1   Client-Server Paradigm

In the *client-server* paradigm (Figure 1-3), a server advertises a set of services that provide access to some *resources* (such as databases). The code that implements these services is hosted locally by the server. We say that the server holds the *know-how*. Finally, it is the server itself that executes the service and thus has the *processor* capability. If the client is interested in accessing a resource hosted by the server, the client will simply use one or more of the services provided by the server. Note that the client needs some "intelligence" to decide which of the services it should use. The server has it all: the know-how, resources, and processor.

So far, most distributed systems have been based on this paradigm. We see it supported by a wide range of technologies such as remote procedure calling, object request brokers (CORBA), and Java remote method invocation (RMI).

1.4.2   Code-on-Demand Paradigm

According to the *code-on-demand* paradigm (Figure 1-4), you first get the know-how when you need it. Suppose that a client initially is unable to execute its task because of a lack of code (know-how). Fortunately, a host in the network provides the needed code. Once the code is received by the client, the computation is carried out in the client. The client holds the processor capability as well as the local resources. In contrast to the classical client-server paradigm, the client does not need preinstalled code because *all* the necessary code will be downloaded. We say that the client has the resources and processor, and the host has the know-how.

Java applets and servlets are excellent practical examples of this paradigm. Applets get downloaded in Web browsers and execute locally, whereas servlets get uploaded to remote Web servers and execute there.

1.4.3   Mobile Agent Paradigm

A key characteristic of the *mobile agent* paradigm (Figure 1-5) is that any host in the network is allowed a high degree of flexibility to possess any mixture of

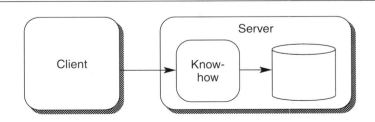

FIGURE 1-3   Client-Server Paradigm

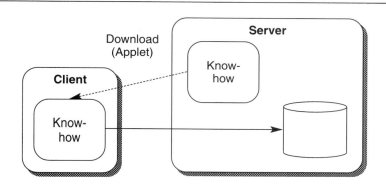

FIGURE 1-4 Code-on-Demand Paradigm

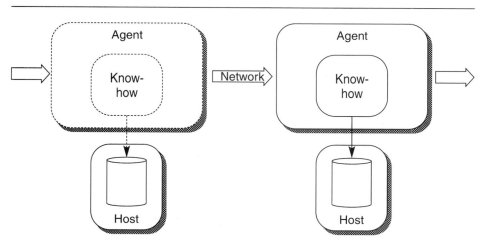

FIGURE 1-5 Mobile Agent Paradigm

know-how, resources, and processors. Its processing capabilities can be combined with local resources. Know-how (in the form of mobile agents) is not tied to a single host but rather is available throughout the network.

If you compare these three paradigms, you will see the chronological trend toward greater flexibility. The client and the server have merged and become a *host*. The applet and the servlet, while serving as client and server extenders, respectively, have been combined and improved with the emergence of mobile agents.

1.5 Mobile Agent Applications

We will now take a closer look at applications that benefit from the mobile agent paradigm. Please note that this is by no means an exhaustive list.

- *Electronic commerce.* Mobile agents are well suited for electronic commerce. A commercial transaction may require real-time access to remote resources such as stock quotes and perhaps even agent-to-agent negotiation. Different agents will have different goals and will implement and exercise different strategies to accomplish these goals. We envision agents that embody the intentions of their creators and act and negotiate on their behalf. Mobile agent technology is a very appealing solution to this kind of problem.

- *Personal assistance.* The mobile agent's ability to execute on remote hosts makes it suitable for playing a role as an assistant capable of performing tasks in the network on behalf of its creator. The remote assistant will operate independently of its limited network connectivity, and the creator can feel free to turn off his or her computer. To schedule a meeting with several other people, a user could send a mobile agent to interact with the representative agents of each of the people invited to the meeting. The agents could negotiate and establish a meeting time.

- *Secure brokering.* An interesting application of mobile agents is in collaborations in which not all the collaborators are trusted. In this case, the parties could let their mobile agents meet on a mutually agreed secure host, where collaboration can take place without the risk of the host taking the side of one of the visiting agents.

- *Distributed information retrieval.* Information retrieval is a popular example of a mobile agent application. Instead of moving large amounts of data to the search engine so that it can create search indexes, you dispatch agents to remote information sources, where they locally create search indexes that can later be shipped back to the origin. Mobile agents can also perform extended searches that are not constrained by the hours during which the creator's computer is operational.

- *Telecommunication networks services.* Support and management of advanced telecommunication services are characterized by dynamic network reconfiguration and user customization. The physical size of these networks and the strict requirements under which they operate call for mobile agent technology to form the glue that keeps such systems flexible yet effective.

- *Workflow applications and groupware.* It is in the nature of workflow applications to support the flow of information between coworkers. The mobile agent is particularly useful here, because in addition to mobility it provides a degree of autonomy to the workflow item. Individual workflow items fully embody the information and behavior they need to move through the organization independently of any particular application.

- *Monitoring and notification.* This classic mobile agent application highlights the asynchronous nature of mobile agents. An agent can monitor a given information source without being dependent on the location from which it originates. Agents can be dispatched to wait for certain kinds of information to become available. It is often important that the life spans of monitoring agents exceed or are independent of the computing processes that create them.

- *Information dissemination.* Mobile agents embody the so-called Internet push model. Agents can disseminate information such as news and automatic software updates for vendors. The agents bring the new software components as well as the installation procedures directly to the customer's personal computer and autonomously update and manage the software on the computer.

- *Parallel processing.* Given that mobile agents can create a cascade of clones in the network, one potential use of mobile agent technology is to administer parallel processing tasks. If a computation requires so much processor power that it must be distributed among multiple processors, an infrastructure of mobile agent hosts could be a plausible way to allocate the processes.

1.6 Application Example: TabiCan

Electronic commerce is one the fields that we expect to benefit from mobile agent technology. In this section we will describe an aglet-based framework that has been used to create a commercial service named TabiCan. (The URL is *www. tabican.ne.jp*. Unfortunately, this service is available only in Japanese.) TabiCan is an electronic marketplace for air tickets and package tours (flight and hotel) and has been designed to host thousands of agents. In the server, shop agents wait for requests from consumer agents. Different shop agents may implement different sales policies, and consumer agents may implement different negotiation strategies. Users visiting this site can leave behind agents that will search for deals for as long as 24 hours.

An IBM team has developed an electronic marketplace framework based on Aglets SDK. An *electronic marketplace* is a multiagent system in which selling and buying agents interact (see Figure 1-6). This architecture redefines the roles of participants: marketplace owners, shop owners, and consumers. The role of market-

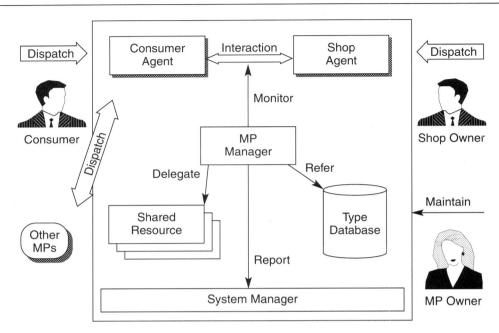

FIGURE 1-6   The Aglet Marketplace

place owners is simply to manage system resources such as hardware and database systems. Users of marketplaces—that is, shop owners and consumers—are responsible for maintaining applications that are implemented as software agents. The framework is developed on top of aglets and is called Aglet Marketplace Middleware (AMPM). An important construct of AMPM is a type database that stores information about the types of messages between agents. The type database enables unfamiliar agents that were independently developed to interact with each other.

From the perspective of electronic marketplace implementation, the agent properties are mobility and messaging. Mobility makes possible the following agent activities in a marketplace:

- Shop agents go to a market from a shop owner's terminal.
- Customer agents travel around various markets to get more information.
- Market advertisers go to other markets to invite customer agents.

Because agents can be developed independently, the agent system is made flexible in the sense that adding a new agent or updating an existing agent can easily modify its behavior. For example, one should be able to replace a shop or a customer agent with an updated agent as long as the new agent behaves in accordance with the defined interaction protocol. When developing the electronic marketplace, the team first implemented a single-market application and then transformed it into a multiple-market configuration. The team members first added a protocol for advertising a market; next, they created a new agent, the Market Advertiser; and finally, they updated the customer agent so that it could move to another market in response to an advertiser's message. The actual modification of the customer agent consisted of the addition of the necessary code for going to another market.

On the basis of the team's observations, we see promising signs that the use of agent technology such as aglets ultimately will lead to a new approach to software development and maintenance. The trend toward improved encapsulation and delegation that was started by object technology will perhaps be taken to new levels by agent technology.

1.7   Contemporary Mobile Agent Systems

What kind of mobile agent systems are available? Fortunately, Java has generated a flood of experimental mobile agent systems. Numerous systems are currently under development, and most of them are available for evaluation on the Web.

The field is developing so dynamically and so fast that any attempt to map agent systems will be outdated before this book goes to press. We will, however, mention a few interesting Java-based mobile agent systems: Aglets, Odyssey, Concordia, and Voyager.

- *Aglets*. This system, created by the authors of this book, mirrors the applet model in Java. The goal was to bring the flavor of mobility to the applet. As we mentioned earlier, the term *aglet* is a portmanteau word combining *agent* and *applet*. We attempted to make aglets an exercise in clean design, and it is our hope that applet programmers will appreciate the many ways in which the aglet model reflects the applet model.

- *Odyssey*. General Magic Inc. invented the mobile agent and created Telescript, the first commercial mobile agent system. Based on a proprietary language and network architecture, Telescript had a short life. In response to the popularity of the Internet and later the steamroller success of the Java language, General Magic decided to reimplement the mobile agent paradigm in its Java-based Odyssey. This system effectively implements the Telescript concepts in the shape of Java classes. The result is a Java class library that enables developers to create their own mobile agent applications.

- *Concordia*. Mitsubishi's Concordia is a framework for the development and management of mobile agent applications that extend to any system supporting Java. Concordia consists of multiple components, all written in Java, which are combined to provide a complete environment for distributed applications. A Concordia system, at its simplest, is made up of a standard Java VM, a server, and a set of agents.

- *Voyager.* ObjectSpace's Voyager is a platform for agent-enhanced distributed computing in Java. While Voyager provides an extensive set of object messaging capabilities, it also allows objects to move as agents in the network. You can say that Voyager combines the properties of a Java-based object request broker with those of a mobile agent system. In this way Voyager allows Java programmers to create network applications using both traditional and agent-enhanced distributed programming techniques.

Note that the Java-based mobile agent systems have a lot in common. In addition to the programming language, all of them rely on standard versions of the Java virtual machine and Java's object serialization mechanism. A common server-based architecture permeates all the systems. Agent transport mechanisms and the support for interaction (messaging) vary a lot.

Although a majority of the contemporary mobile agent systems are based on the Java language system, you will also find other languages in use. The most significant languages are Tcl, Scheme, and Python.

- *Agent Tcl.* Dartmouth College's Agent Tcl is a mobile agent system whose agents can be written in Tcl. It has extensive navigation and communication services, security mechanisms, and debugging and tracking tools. The main component of Agent Tcl is a server that runs on each machine and that allows the entire execution state, including local variables and instruction pointer, to move. When an agent wants to migrate to a new machine, it calls a single function, `agent_jump`, which automatically captures the complete state of the agent and sends this state information to the server on the destination machine. The destination server starts up a Tcl execution, loads the state information into this execution environment, and restarts the agent from the exact point where it left off.

- *Ara.* Tcl-based Ara, from University of Kaiserslautern, is a platform for the portable and secure execution of mobile agents in heterogeneous networks. The research project is primarily concerned with system support for general mobile agents to ensure secure and portable execution and much less concerned with application-level features of agents, such as agent cooperation patterns, intelligent behavior, and user modeling.

- *TACOMA.* The University of Tromsø and Cornell University project (TACOMA) focuses on operating system support for agents and ways agents can be used to solve problems traditionally addressed by operating systems. The TACOMA system is based on UNIX and the Transmission Control Protocol (TCP). The system supports agents written in C, Tcl/Tk, Perl, Python, and Scheme (Elk). The system itself is implemented in C.

A number of the Tcl-based projects anticipate a move toward support for multiple languages, something that essentially means added support for Java.

We recommend the following Web sites for more information on the specific agent systems and projects:

- Aglets at *www.tr1.ibm.co.jp/aglets*
- Odyssey at *www.generalmagic.com/technology.technology.html*
- Concordia at *www.meitca.com/HSL/Projects/Concordia*
- Voyager at *www.objectspace.com/voyager*
- Agent Tcl at *www.cs.dartmouth.edu/~agent*
- Ara at *www.uni-kl.de/AG-Nehmer/Projekte/Ara*
- TACOMA at *www.cs.uit.no/DOS/Tacoma*

1.8   Mobile Agent Standardization: MASIF

Let us conclude this chapter with a brief overview of ongoing standardization efforts in the mobile agent field.

Clearly, the systems mentioned earlier differ widely in architecture and implementation, thereby impeding interoperability and rapid deployment of mobile agent technology in the marketplace. To promote interoperability, some aspects of mobile agent technology must be standardized. Five companies—Crystaliz, General Magic Inc., GMD Fokus, IBM Corporation, and the Open Group—have jointly developed a proposal for a Mobile Agent System Interoperability Facility (MASIF) and brought it to the attention of the Object Management Group (OMG).

MASIF addresses the interfaces between agent systems and not between agent applications and agent systems. Even though the former seems to be more relevant for application developers, it is the latter that allows mobile agents to travel across multiple hosts in an open environment. Clearly, MASIF is not about language interoperability. Language interoperability for mobile objects is very difficult, and MASIF is limited to interoperability between agent systems written in the same language but potentially by different vendors. Furthermore, MASIF does not attempt to standardize local agent operations such as agent interpretation, serialization, or execution. You can say that MASIF defines the interfaces at the agent system level rather than at the agent level.

MASIF standardizes the following four areas:

- *Agent management.* There is interest in the mobile agent community in standardizing agent management. It is clearly desirable that a system administrator who manages agent systems of different types be able to use the same standard operations. It should be possible to find agents, to create an agent given a class name for the agent, to suspend an agent's execution, to resume its execution, or to terminate it in a standard way.

- *Agent transfer.* It is desirable that agent applications be able to spawn agents that can move freely among agent systems of different types, resulting in a common infrastructure.

- *Agent and agent system names.* In addition to standardizing operations for interoperability between agent systems, the syntax and semantics of various parameters must be standardized. Specifically, agent names and agent system names should be standardized. This would allow agent systems and agents to identify each other and would allow applications to identify agents and agent systems.

- *Agent system type and location syntax.* The location syntax must be standardized to allow an agent to access agent system type information from a desired destination agent system. The agent transfer can happen only if the destination agent system type can support the agent. Location syntax also must be standardized so that agent systems can locate each other.

1.9   Summary

In this chapter we defined an agent as a software object that is situated within an execution environment and is reactive, autonomous, goal-driven, and temporally continuous. An agent may also be communicative, mobile, capable of learning, and believable.

We defined a mobile agent as an agent that is not bound to the system where it begins execution. It has the unique ability to transport itself from one system in a network to another. This ability allows a mobile agent to move to a system that contains an object with which the agent wants to interact and then to take advantage of being in the same host or network as the object. We gave you seven good reasons to start using mobile agents: they reduce the network load, they overcome network latency, they encapsulate protocols, they execute asynchronously and autonomously, they adapt dynamically, they are naturally heterogeneous, and they are robust and fault-tolerant.

We discussed a number of application domains that benefit from mobile agent technology, including electronic commerce, personal assistance, secure brokering, distributed information retrieval, telecommunication network services, workflow applications and groupware, monitoring and notification, information dissemination, and parallel processing.

In a case history from the field of electronic commerce, we described how an aglet-based framework has been used to create a commercial service named Tabi-

Can. This actual aglet-based application has been designed to host thousands of agents.

We also looked at several Java-based mobile agent systems: aglets, Odyssey, Concordia, Voyager, and many more. Although these Java-based mobile agent systems have a lot in common, they do not interoperate. To promote interoperability, some aspects of mobile agent technology have been standardized by OMG's MASIF. It will be interesting to see what impact increased standardization activities will have on the mobile agent field.

In Chapter 2 we will discuss in greater detail the elements that make up a mobile agent system as well as the essentials of mobile agent behavior.

Chapter 2

Elements of a Mobile Agent System

After reading this chapter you should have a basic understanding of the elements of a mobile agent system. You will first learn about the basic conceptual model of mobile agents, which is based on two core concepts: agent and place. After creating a solid conceptual foundation we will go on to cover the essentials of agent behavior: the creation and disposal of agents, their transfer over a network, and agent communication concepts. We will conclude this chapter with a brief overview of the MASIF standard.

2.1 Agent and Place

The two fundamental concepts in the mobile agent model are the *agent* and its execution environment, which we term the *place*. Let us start with the agent.

2.1.1 Agent

A mobile agent is an entity that has five attributes: state, implementation, interface, identifier, and principals (see Figure 2-1). When an agent moves in the network it takes these attributes along with it.

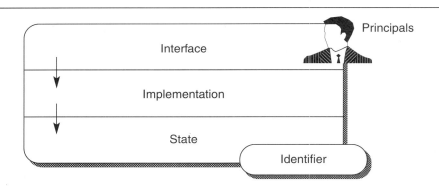

FIGURE 2-1   Agent Properties

- *State:* needed for the agent to resume computation after traveling.
- *Implementation:* needed for location-independent agent execution.
- *Interface:* needed for agent communication.
- *Identifier:* needed to recognize and locate traveling agents.
- *Principals:* needed to determine legal and moral responsibility.

In this chapter we make the basic assumption that agents are constructed according to the principles of object-oriented programming. We use object terminology extensively to describe mobile agent concepts. We expect our readers to be well versed in object-oriented programming and to understand terms such as *class*, *instantiation*, *state*, and *instance variable*.

State   When an agent travels, it transports its state with it. It must do so in order to resume execution at the destination host, a characteristic of virtually all mobile agents. The agent's state at any given time is a snapshot of its execution. For most programming languages we can partition the agent's state into its *execution state*, which is its runtime state (including its program counter and frame stack), and its *object state*, which is the value of the instance variables in the object.

Agents are not always required to capture and transport their execution state with them in order to resume execution at the destination host. In many cases an approximation will be sufficient. The values of the instance variables can help the agent to determine what to do when it resumes execution at its destination. As we will see later, this is an approximation appropriate for Java-based agents that generally cannot access their execution state. The Java language does not provide access to stack information; even if it did, the differences in stack representations between Java virtual machines would make it impractical to successfully transfer execution state in a heterogeneous environment.

Implementation Like any other computer program, a mobile agent needs code in order to execute. When it travels, it has the option of either taking its implementation code or going to the destination, seeing what code is already there, and retrieving any missing code over the network (code-on-demand).

The agent implementation should be both executable at the destination host and safe for the host to execute. Scripting and interpreted languages offer platform independence as well as a controlled execution environment featuring a security mechanism that restricts access to the host's private resources.

Interface An agent provides an interface that allows other agents and systems to interact with it. This interface can be anything from a set of method signatures that allow other agents and applications to access methods on the agent to a messaging interface that allows agents to communicate in "agentspeak" such as the Knowledge Query and Manipulation Language (KQML).

KQML is a language for communication between agents. KQML offers a variety of message types, also known as *performatives*, that express an attitude regarding the content of the exchange. Performatives can also assist agents to process their requests. KQML and its syntax and semantics exist at a level above the agent communication infrastructure described later in this chapter. The infrastructure we describe is not biased toward any specific agent language but rather describes a set of fundamental communication mechanisms that allows point-to-point communication between agents.

Identifier Every agent has an identifier that is unique during its lifetime (immutable). Agents require identities so that they can be identified and located via, for example, directory services. For example, the identifier can be a conjunction of the principals' identities and a serial number. Because an agent's identifier is globally unique and immutable, it can be used as a key in operations that require a way of referring to a particular agent instance.

Principals A principal is an entity whose identity can be authenticated by any system that the principal may try to access. A principal can be an individual, an organization, or a corporation. An identity consists of a name and possibly other attributes. For agents we find at least two main principals:

- *Manufacturer:* the author (i.e., the provider of the agent implementation)
- *Owner:* the principal that has the legal and moral responsibility for the agent's behavior (i.e., the creator of the aglet)

2.1.2 Place

Now that we have defined the primary agent attributes, we are ready to describe the environment in which agents operate. Let us begin by stating that agents, not surprisingly, travel between places. The most common view of a place is that it is a context in which an agent can execute (see Figure 2-2). You can regard it as an entry point for a visiting agent that wishes to execute. The place provides a uniform set of services that the agent can rely on irrespective of its specific location. You can regard the place as the operating system for the agent. Four concepts play an important role in places:

- *Engine:* workhorse and virtual machine for one or more places
- *Resources:* databases, processors, and other services provided by the host
- *Location:* the network address of a given place
- *Principals:* those legally responsible for the operation of a place

Engine   Places cannot themselves execute agents. To do that, agents must reside inside an engine. We use the term *engine* to reflect the fact that the engine serves as the workhorse or virtual machine for places and their agents. It also provides places and agents with links to the underlying network and other resources provided by the host. In this model, an engine is more a physical entity than a concept. In a Java-based mobile agent system, the engine is likely to be identical with the Java virtual machine *and* the operating systems. We will discuss that issue in later chapters.

The engine defines a hierarchical structure (see Figure 2-3). A given computer in a network can host multiple engines; each engine holds multiple places, and each place contains multiple agents. The fact that an engine can contain more than one place requires that places have unique names within an engine. Some

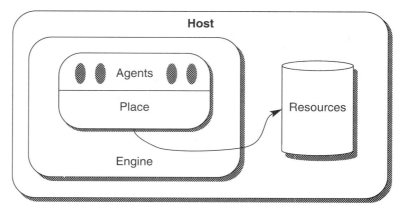

FIGURE 2-2   Place and Engine

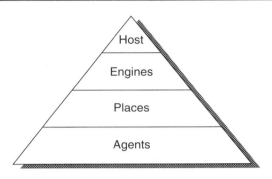

FIGURE 2-3   The Agent Model Pyramid

agent systems may not have an explicit place concept. In such systems you should regard the engine itself as a sort of place.

Resources Together, the engine and the place provide controlled access to local resources and services such as networks, databases, processors and memory, disks, and other hardware as well as software services.

Location Location is an important concept for mobile agents. We define the location of an executing agent as the combination of the name of the place in which it executes and the network address of the engine in which that place resides. This location will typically be written as an Internet Protocol (IP) address and a port of the engine with a place name attribute.

Principals Like an agent, a place has two principals. A place is associated with authorities that identify the person or organization for which the place acts (place master) as well as the manufacturer of the place. The *manufacturer* is the author (provider) of the place implementation, and the *place master* is the principal that has the responsibility for the operation of the place.

2.2   Agent Behavior: Creation and Disposal

Now that we have defined the basic concepts of the agent model, we can move on to the behaviors associated with the creation and transfer of agents. First, let's look at creation and disposal.

An agent gets created in a place. The creation can be initiated either by another agent residing in the same place or by another agent or nonagent system outside the place. The creator is required to authenticate itself to the place, establishing the authority and credentials that the new agent will possess. The creator can also supply initialization arguments for the agent. The class definition needed to instantiate the agent can be present on the local host or a remote host or, if necessary, can be provided by the creator. Creation involves three steps:

1. *Instantiation and identifier assignment.* The class definition (implementation) is loaded and made executable, and the agent object is instantiated. The agent class specifies both the interface and the implementation of the agent. The place assigns a unique identifier to the agent.

2. *Initialization.* The agent is given a chance to initialize itself using any initialization arguments provided by the creator. Only when the initialization has been completed can the agent assume that it has been fully and correctly installed in the place.

3. *Autonomous execution.* After being fully installed in the place, the agent starts execution. It is now capable of executing independently of other agents in the same place.

How does an agent end its life? Most likely it gets disposed of in a place. The disposal can be initiated by the agent itself, by another agent residing in the same place, or by another agent or nonagent system outside the place. An agent can also be disposed of by the system for one of the following reasons:

- End of lifetime: the given lifetime of the agent has expired.
- No use: no one refers to or uses the agent.
- Security violation: the agent has violated the security rules.
- Shutdown: the system is shutting down.

Disposing of an agent is a two-step process:

1. *Preparing for disposal.* The agent is given a chance to finalize its current task before it is disposed of.

2. *Suspension of execution.* The place suspends the execution of the agent.

2.3 Agent Behavior: Transfer

The transfer process can be initiated by the agent itself, by another agent residing in the same place, or by another agent or nonagent system outside the place. The agent is then dispatched from its current place (origin) and received by the specified place (destination).

The origin place and the destination place manage the dispatch process. When the origin place contacts the destination place, the destination place can either fulfill the travel request or return a failure indication to the origin. If the origin place cannot contact the destination place, it must return a failure indication to the agent.

We will now describe the agent transfer process from the viewpoint of the origin as well as that of the destination. This description will be followed by a more detailed discussion of particular issues related to the transfer of agent classes (see Figure 2-4).

2.3.1   Dispatching an Agent

When a mobile agent is preparing for a trip, it must be able to identify its destination. If the place is not specified, the agent runs in a default place selected by the destination agent system. Once the location of the destination is established, the mobile agent informs the local agent system that it wants to transfer itself to the destination agent system. This message is relayed via an internal API between the agent and the agent system (e.g., (go())). When the agent system receives the agent's trip request, it should do the following:

1. *Suspend the agent.* The agent is warned about the imminent transfer and is allowed to prepare for departure (complete its current task). When that is done, its execution thread is halted.

2. *Serialize the agent.* The agent—that is, its state and the agent class—is serialized by the engine. *Serialization* is the process of creating a persistent repre-

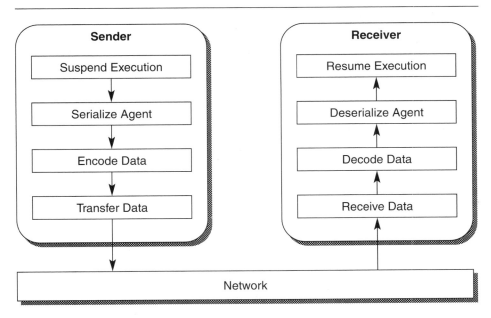

FIGURE 2-4   Agent Transfer

sentation of the agent object that can be transported over a network. Serialization of the agent may include the execution state (stack frames).

3. *Encode the serialized agent.* The engine now encodes the serialized agent for the chosen transport protocol.

4. *Transfer the agent.* The engine establishes a network connection to the specified destination host and transfers the encoded serialized agent.

2.3.2   Receiving an Agent

Before an engine receives an agent, the engine must determine whether it can accept an agent from the sending host. Only after the sender has successfully authenticated itself to the receiving engine will the actual data transfer take place:

1. Receive the agent: when the destination engine agrees to the transfer, the encoded agent is received.

2. Decode the agent: the engine decodes the incoming data stream.

3. Deserialize the agent: the persistent representation of the agent is deserialized. The agent class is instantiated, and the transferred agent state is restored.

4. Resume agent execution: the re-created agent is notified of its arrival at the destination place. It can now prepare to resume its execution and is given a new thread of execution.

2.3.3   Agent Class Transfer

The agent cannot resume execution in the destination engine without its class being present. Fortunately, there are several ways to make the class available for the destination engine, depending on the location of the class:

- *Class at destination.* If the class is already available at the destination, either in the engine's class cache or in the local file system, there is no need to transfer the class (see Figure 2-5a). The transferred agent need contain only the information required to identify the class, such as the full class name and discriminator. It may also contain additional information that describes the location of the class definition.

- *Class at origin.* If the class is located at the origin, as will often be the case, it can easily be transported with the agent's state to the destination engine (see Figure 2-5b). Observe, however, that classes in this scheme can easily get transported to the destination engine more than once, perhaps leading to increased network traffic and wasted network bandwidth.

- *Code-on-demand.* In this case, the class is available from a server and the destination engine can retrieve the class on a code-on-demand basis (see Fig-

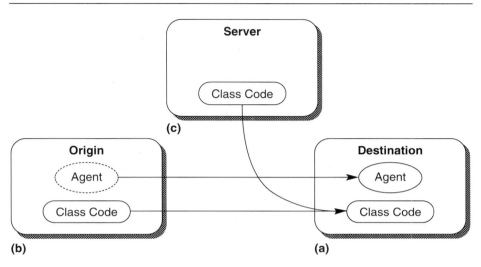

FIGURE 2-5   Agent Class Transfer: (a) Class at Destination, (b) Class
at Origin, (c) Class at Server

ure 2-5c). Note that the destination engine in this case must perform an additional network connection to retrieve the class.

After an agent has been instantiated, it often creates other objects. Clearly, the classes of these objects are needed for their instantiation and continued execution. If any of these classes is not available at the destination engine, it must be transferred either from the origin or the sender of the agent. There is a choice of policies for transfer of auxiliary classes. Either the agent can decide to bring all the needed classes in the first place, or auxiliary classes can be brought on a per-request basis.

2.4   Communication

Agents can communicate with other agents residing within the same place (intraplace) or with agents residing in other places (interplace and interengine). An agent can invoke a method of another agent or send it a message if it is authorized to do so. In general, agent messaging can be peer-to-peer or broadcast. Broadcasting is a one-to-many messaging scheme. It allows a single agent to post a message to a group of agents (subscribers) and is a useful mechanism in multi-agent systems.

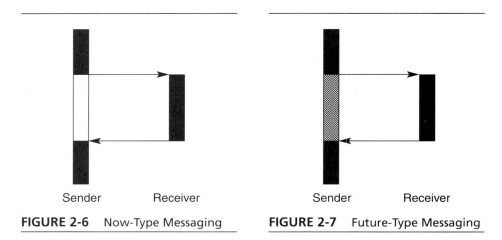

FIGURE 2-6   Now-Type Messaging   **FIGURE 2-7**   Future-Type Messaging

Interagent communication can follow three different schemes:

- *Now-type messaging.* This is the most popular and commonly used messaging scheme. A now-type message is synchronous and blocks further execution until the receiver of the message has completed the handling of the message and replied to it (see Figure 2-6).

- *Future-type messaging.* A future-type message is asynchronous and does not block the current execution (see Figure 2-7). The sender retains a handle (a future), which can be used to obtain the result. Because the sender does not have to wait until the receiver responds and sends the reply, this messaging scheme is flexible and is particularly useful when multiple agents communicate with one another.

- *One-way-type messaging.* A one-way-type message is asynchronous and does not block the current execution (see Figure 2-8). The sender will not retain a handle for this message, and the receiver will never have to reply to it. This messaging scheme is convenient when two agents are allowed to engage in a loosely connected conversation in which the message-sending agent does not expect any replies from the message-receiving agent. You will sometimes also see this scheme termed *fire-and-forget*.

2.5   MASIF: `MAFAgentSystem` and `MAFFinder`

Let us conclude this chapter by returning to the Mobile Agent System Interoperability Facility. MASIF is a collection of definitions and interfaces that provides an

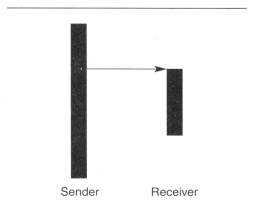

Sender   Receiver

FIGURE 2-8   One-Way-Type Messaging

interoperable interface for mobile agent systems. MASIF has been kept as simple and generic as possible to allow for future advances in the emerging mobile agent field.

We have discussed reasons for standardizing certain areas of mobile agent technology. Now let's look briefly at the two core components (actually, interfaces) of the MASIF specification: MAFAgentSystem and MAFFinder.

The MAFAgentSystem interface defines operations for creation, management, and transfer of agents. The MAFFinder interface defines operations for registering, unregistering, and locating agents, places, and agent systems.

Common Object Request Broker Architecture (CORBA) is the Object Management Group's (OMG) language-neutral and platform-independent standard for distributed object systems. MASIF can use services provided by CORBA, including the naming service, lifecycle service, externalization service, and security service. The relationship with CORBA simplifies MASIF. For example, MASIF does not specify remote interaction with agents and agent systems. In MASIF, the agent system is a CORBA object. Client applications can access these agent system objects (or they can access each other) through their CORBA interfaces (see Figure 2-9). MASIF does *not* specify the nature of agent objects. Visit OMG's Web site for more information about CORBA and MASIF (*www.omg.org*).

2.5.1 The MAFAgentSystem Interface

The MAFAgentSystem interface defines methods and objects that support agent management tasks such as fetching an agent system name and receiving an agent. These methods and objects provide a basic set of operations for agent transfer. The interface is shown here in the Interface Description Language (IDL), which is the

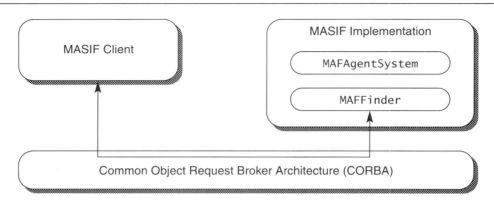

FIGURE 2-9   The Relationship between MASIF and CORBA ORB

programming-language-independent interface specification language used by OMG. If you are familiar with Java, C, or C++, it should speak for itself.

```
interface MAFAgentSystem {
    void create_agent(
        in Name agent_name,
        in AgentProfile agent_profile,
        in OctetString agent,
        in string place_name,
        in Arguments arguments,
        in ClassNameList class_names,
        in string code_base,
        in MAFAgentSystem class_provider
    ) raises (ClassUnknown, ArgumentInvalid, SerializationFailed,
            MAFExtendedException);
    OctetStrings fetch_class(
        in ClassNameList class_name_list,
        in string code_base,
        in AgentProfile agent_profile
    ) raises (ClassUnknown, MAFExtendedException);
    Location find_nearby_agent_system_of_profile (
        in AgentProfile profile
    ) raises (EntryNotFound);
    AgentStatus get_agent_status(
        in Name agent_name
    ) raises (NameInvalid);
    AgentSystemInfo get_agent_system_info();
    AuthInfo get_authinfo(
        in Name agent_name
    ) raises (NameInvalid);
    MAFFinder get_MAFFinder() raises (FinderNotFound);
    NameList list_all_agents();
```

```
            NameList list_all_agents_of_authority(
                in Authority authority);
            Locations list_all_places();
            void receive_agent(
                in Name agent_name,
                in AgentProfile agent_profile,
                in OctetString agent,
                in string place_name,
                in ClassNameList class_names,
                in string code_base,
                in MAFAgentSystem agent_sender
            ) raises (ClassUnknown, ArgumentInvalid, DeserializationFailed,
                    MAFExtendedException);
            void resume_agent(
                in Name agent_name
            ) raises (NameInvalid, ResumeFailed);
            void suspend_agent(
                in Name agent_name
            ) raises (NameInvalid, SuspendFailed);
            void terminate_agent(
                in Name agent_name
            ) raises (NameInvalid, TerminateFailed);
            void terminate_agent_system() raises (TerminationFailed);
        };
```

2.5.2   The MAFFinder Interface

The CORBA services are designed for static objects. When CORBA services, such as the naming service, are applied to mobile agents, they may not handle all cases well. Therefore, a MAFFinder interface is also included in MASIF. It functions as an interface of a dynamic name and location database of agents, places, and agent systems.

MAFFinder is actually an agent naming service. Before a client can ask MAFFinder to find an object, the client must obtain the object reference to MAFFinder. To get it, the client can use either the CORBA naming service or the internal interfaces provided by the agent system to actually access the get_MAFFinder method in the MAFAgentSystem interface. Again we show the interface in IDL.

```
            interface MAFFinder {
                void register_agent(
                    in Name agent_name,
                    in Location agent_location,
                    in AgentProfile agent_profile
                ) raises (NameInvalid);
                void register_agent_system(
                    in Name agent_system_name,
                    in Location agent_system_location,
                    in AgentSystemInfo agent_system_info
                ) raises (NameInvalid);
```

```
void register_place(
    in string place_name,
    in Location place_location
) raises (NameInvalid);
Locations lookup_agent(
    in Name agent_name,
    in AgentProfile agent_profile
) raises (EntryNotFound);
Locations lookup_agent_system(
    in Name agent_system_name,
    in AgentSystemInfo agent_system_info
) raises (EntryNotFound);
Location lookup_place(in string place_name
) raises (EntryNotFound);
void unregister_agent(in Name agent_name
) raises (EntryNotFound);
void unregister_agent_system(in Name agent_system_name
) raises (EntryNotFound);
void unregister_place(in string place_name
) raises (EntryNotFound);
};
```

2.6   Summary

This chapter introduced the two fundamental concepts in the mobile agent model: agent and place. A mobile agent is an entity having five attributes: state, implementation, interface, identifier, and principals; a place is a context in which agents can execute. The place provides a uniform set of services that the agent can rely on irrespective of its specific location.

An agent gets created in a place. The creation can be initiated either by another agent residing in the same place or by another agent or nonagent system outside the place. Creation involves three steps: instantiation and identifier assignment; initialization; and autonomous execution. An agent also gets disposed of in a place. The disposal can be initiated by the agent itself, by another agent residing in the same place, or by another agent or nonagent system outside the place. Disposing of an agent is a two-step process: preparing for disposal and suspension of execution.

When a mobile agent is preparing for a trip, it must be able to identify its destination. Once the location of the destination is established, the mobile agent informs the local agent system that it wants to transfer itself to the destination agent system. When the agent system receives the agent's trip request, it should suspend the agent, serialize the agent, encode the serialized agent, and finally transfer the agent. Before an engine receives an agent, the engine must determine whether it can accept an agent from the sending host. Only after the sender has successfully authenticated itself to the receiving engine will the actual data transfer take place: receiving the agent, decoding the agent, deserializing the agent, and resuming agent execution.

Agents can communicate with other agents residing within the same place (intraplace) or with agents residing in other places (interplace and interengine). In general, agent messaging can be peer-to-peer or broadcast. Interagent communication can follow three different schemes: now-type messaging, future-type messaging, or one-way-type messaging.

We concluded this chapter with a description of the Mobile Agent System Interoperability Facility standard. MASIF is a collection of definitions and interfaces that provides an interoperable interface for mobile agent systems. MASIF standardizes agent operations, including receiving, creating, suspending, and terminating; as well as operations for registering, unregistering, and locating agents, places, and agent systems.

In Chapter 3 we will turn to the specific mobile agent that is the subject of this book: the aglet, or Java-based mobile agent.

Chapter 3

Mobile Agents
with Java

You probably already know what Java is. The language that changed the Web overnight offers unique capabilities that are fueling the development of mobile agent systems. In this chapter we will show what it is that makes Java a powerful tool for agent development. We will also direct your attention to some shortcomings in Java language systems that have implications for the design and use of Java-based mobile agent systems.

This chapter will also introduce you to the *aglet*, a Java-based mobile agent. A brief overview of the aglet and its API will link the mobile agent model presented in Chapter 2 with Java. The remaining chapters will be dedicated to particular elements of the Aglet API.

3.1   Agent Characteristics of Java: Benefits

Java is an object-oriented, network-savvy programming language. Some people call it a "better C++," one that omits many rarely used, confusing features of C++. Others call it the language of the Internet. We think of Java primarily as an excellent vehicle for mobile agents. Let us look at some of the properties of Java that make it a good language for mobile agent programming.

3.1.1   Platform Independence

Java is designed to operate in heterogeneous environments. To enable a Java application to execute anywhere on the network, the compiler generates architecture-neutral byte code as opposed to nonportable native code. For this code to be executed on a given computer, the Java runtime system must be present. The Java language has no platform-dependent aspects. Primitive data types are rigorously specified and are not dependent on the underlying processor or operating system. Even libraries are platform-independent parts of the system. For example, the window library provides a single interface for the GUI that is independent of the underlying operating system. It allows us to create a mobile agent without knowing the types of computers it is going to run on.

3.1.2   Secure Execution

Java is intended for use on the Internet and intranets, and the demand for security has influenced the design in several ways. For example, Java has a pointer model that eliminates the possibility of overwriting memory and corrupting data. Java simply does not allow illegal type casting or any pointer arithmetic. Programs are no longer able to forge access to private data in objects that they do not have access to, an arrangement that prevents a certain category of viruses. Even if someone tampers with the byte code, the Java runtime system ensures that the code will not be able to violate the basic semantics of Java. Java also has a security manager to check all potentially unsafe operations, such as file access and network connections, to determine whether the given program is permitted to perform these operations. Overall, the security architecture of Java makes it reasonably safe to host an untrusted agent, because it cannot tamper with the host or access private information.

3.1.3   Dynamic Class Loading

This mechanism allows the virtual machine to load and define classes at runtime. It provides a protective name space for each agent, thus allowing agents to execute safely and independently of each other. The class-loading mechanism is extensible and enables classes to be loaded via the network.

3.1.4   Multithread Programming

Agents are by definition autonomous; an agent executes independently of other agents residing within the same place. Allowing each agent to execute in its own lightweight process, also called a *thread of execution*, is a way of enabling agents to behave autonomously. Fortunately, Java not only allows multithread programming but also supports a set of synchronization primitives that are built into the language. These primitives enable agent interaction.

3.1.5   Object Serialization

A key feature of mobile agents is that they can be serialized and deserialized. Java conveniently provides a built-in serialization mechanism that can represent the state of an object in a serialized form sufficiently detailed for the object to be reconstructed later. The serialized form of the object must be able to identify the Java class from which the object's state was saved and to restore the state in a new instance. Objects often refer to other objects. To maintain the object structure, these other objects must be stored and retrieved at the same time. When an object is stored, all the objects in the graph that are reachable from that object are also stored.

3.1.6   Reflection

Java code can discover information about the fields, methods, and constructors of loaded classes and can use reflected fields, methods, and constructors to operate on their underlying counterparts in objects, all within the security restrictions. Reflection accommodates the need for agents to be smart about themselves and other agents.

3.2   Agent Characteristics of Java: Drawbacks

Although the Java language system is highly suitable for creating mobile agents, we should be aware of some significant shortcomings. Some of them can be worked around; others are more serious and have implications for the overall conceptual design and deployment of Java-based mobile agent systems.

3.2.1   Inadequate Support for Resource Control

The Java language system provides no means for us to control the resources consumed by a Java object. For example, an agent can start looping and waste processor cycles, and it can also start consuming memory resources. These two examples relate to a specific type of security attack termed *denial of service*. In one of the most feared types of attack by mobile agents, agents swarm into a computer and take over all its resources, making it impossible for the operator to control the computer. Unfortunately, Java provides no way for the host to limit the processor and memory resources allocated by a given object or thread.

A related issue (which actually goes beyond Java) is the ability of the agent to allocate resources external to the program, for example by opening files and sockets and creating windows. The agent's allocation of these resources can be controlled, but once the agent is disposed of or dispatched to another host these resources must be released. However, it is difficult to do so, because Java provides no support for binding such resources to a specific object. So we may see a mobile agent that "forgets" its GUI and leaves behind an open window on our display when it leaves for another host.

3.2.2   No Protection of References

A Java object's public methods are available to any other object that has a reference to it. Because there is no concept of a protected reference, some objects are allowed access to a larger set of public methods in the Java object's interface than others are. This access is important for the agent. There is no way that the agent can directly monitor and control which other agents are accessing its methods.

We have found that a practical and powerful solution to this problem is to insert a *proxy* object between the caller and the callee to control access. This approach not only provides protection of references but also offers a solution to the problem mentioned next and provides location transparency in general (explained later).

3.2.3   No Object Ownership of References

No one owns the references to a given object in Java. For an agent, this means that we can take its thread of execution away from it, but we cannot explicitly void the agent (object) itself. This is a task for the automated garbage collector. At present, the garbage collector will not reclaim any object until all references to the object have been voided. So if some other agent has a reference to our agent, it will unavoidably open a loophole for that agent to keep *our* agent alive against our will. All we can do is to repeat the warning against giving away direct references to agents in Java. The forthcoming Java Development Kit (JDK) 1.2 provides support for weak reference, which will solve this problem.

3.2.4   No Support for Preservation and Resumption of the Execution State

It is currently impossible in Java to retrieve the full execution state of an object. Information such as the status of the program counter and frame stack is permanently forbidden territory for Java programs. Therefore, for a mobile agent to properly resume a computation on a remote host, it must rely on internal attribute values and external events to direct it. An embedded automaton can keep track of the agent's travels and ensure that computations are properly halted and properly resumed.

3.3   Mobile Java Agent: The Aglet Model

Now let us introduce you to the *aglet* object model. This model was designed to benefit from the agent characteristics of Java while overcoming some of the deficiencies in the language system. In the aglet object model, a mobile agent is a mobile object that has its own thread of control, is event-driven, and communicates by message passing.

3.3.1   Basic Elements

Now let us take a closer look at the model underlying the Aglet API. This model defines a set of abstractions and the behavior needed to leverage mobile agent technology in Internet-like, open wide-area networks. The key abstractions are aglet, proxy, context, and identifier:

- *Aglet.* An aglet is a mobile Java object that visits aglet-enabled hosts in a computer network. It is autonomous, because it runs in its own thread of execution after arriving at a host, and reactive, because it can respond to incoming messages.

- *Proxy.* A proxy is a representative of an aglet. It serves as a shield that protects the aglet from direct access to its public methods (see Figure 3-1). The proxy also provides location transparency for the aglet; that is, it can hide the aglet's real location. This means that an aglet and its proxies can be separated so that a local proxy hides the remoteness of the aglet.

- *Context.* A context is an aglet's workplace. It closely corresponds to the *place* concept introduced in Chapter 2. It is a stationary object that provides a means for maintaining and managing running aglets in a uniform execution environment where the host system is secured against malicious aglets (see Figure 3-2). One node in a computer network may run multiple server processes (*engines*), and each server may host multiple contexts. Contexts are named and thus can be located by the combination of their server's address and their name.

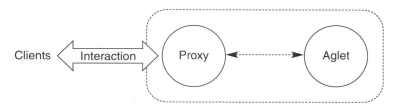

FIGURE 3-1   Relationship between Aglet and Proxy

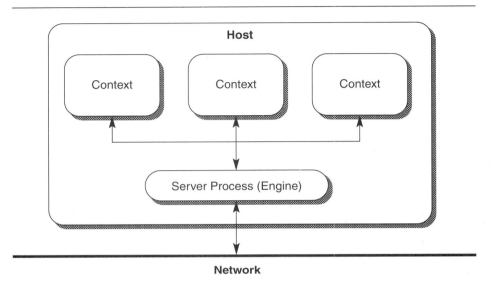

FIGURE 3-2   Relationship between Host, Server Process (Engine),
and Contexts

- *Identifier.* An identifier is bound to each aglet. This identifier is globally unique and immutable throughout the lifetime of the aglet.

Behavior supported by the aglet object model is based on a careful analysis of the life and death of mobile agents. There are basically only two ways to bring an aglet to life: either it is instantiated from scratch (creation) or it is copied from an existing aglet (cloning). To control the population of aglets you can of course destroy them (disposal). Aglets are mobile in two different ways: actively and passively. The active approach is characterized by an aglet pushing itself from its current host to a remote host (dispatching). A remote host pulling an aglet away from its current host (retracting) characterizes the passive type of aglet mobility. When aglets are running, they take up resources. To reduce their resource consumption, aglets can go to sleep temporarily, releasing their resources (deactivation), and later can be brought back into running mode (activation). Finally, multiple aglets can exchange information to accomplish a given task (messaging).

This is the minimum set of operations required to create and manage a distributed mobile agent environment. When we created the Aglet API, one of our goals was to create a lightweight API that would be both easy to learn to use and sufficiently comprehensive and robust for real applications. It is tempting to call the Aglet API the RISC of mobile agents.

The following list summarizes the fundamental operations of an aglet: creation, cloning, dispatching, retraction, deactivation, activation, and disposal (see Figure 3-3).

- *Creation.* The creation of an aglet takes place in a context. The new aglet is assigned an identifier, inserted into the context, and initialized. The aglet starts executing as soon as it has been successfully initialized.

- *Cloning.* The cloning of an aglet produces an almost identical copy of the original aglet in the same context. The only differences are the assigned identifier and the fact that execution restarts in the new aglet. Note that execution threads are not cloned.

- *Dispatching.* Dispatching an aglet from one context to another will remove it from its current context and insert it into the destination context, where it will restart execution (execution threads do not migrate). We say that the aglet has been "pushed" to its new context.

- *Retraction.* The retraction of an aglet will pull (remove) it from its current context and insert it into the context from which the retraction was requested.

- *Activation and deactivation.* The deactivation of an aglet is the ability to temporarily halt its execution and store its state in secondary storage. Activation of an aglet will restore it in the same context.

- *Disposal.* The disposal of an aglet will halt its current execution and remove it from its current context.

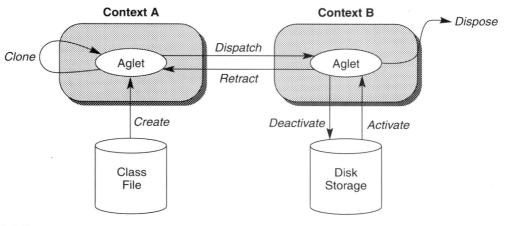

FIGURE 3-3   Aglet Life-Cycle Model

3.3.2   The Aglet Event Model

The aglet programming model is event-based. The model allows the programmer to "plug in" customized *listeners* into an aglet (see Figure 3-4). Listeners catch particular events in the life cycle of an aglet and allow the programmer to take action, for example, when the aglet is being dispatched.

Three kinds of listeners exist:

- *Clone listener:* listens for cloning events. You can customize this listener to take specific actions when an aglet is about to be cloned, when the clone is actually created, and after the cloning has taken place.

- *Mobility listener:* Listens for mobility events. You can use this listener to take action when an aglet is about to be dispatched to another context, when it is about to be retracted from a context, and when it actually arrives in a new context.

- *Persistence listener:* Listens for persistent events. This listener allows the programmer to take action when an aglet is about to be deactivated and after it has been activated.

The `BoomerangItinerary` is an example of a *reusable* listener. It can be plugged into *any* aglet for which we want a boomerang effect. That is, an aglet that always comes back to you no matter where you send it. The `BoomerangItinerary` implements three methods: `onDispatching`, `onArrival`, and `onRetract`. It is `onArrival()` that ensures that the aglet returns home (`origin`) after it has visited the remote server.

```
public class BoomerangItinerary implements MobilityListener {
    Aglet target = null;
    String origin = null;
```

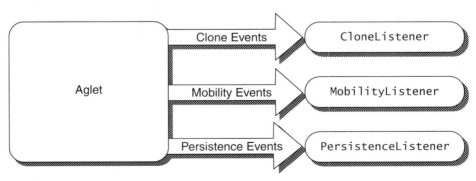

FIGURE 3-4   Relationship between the Aglet and Its Listeners

```
public BoomerangItinerary (Aglet target) {
   target.addMobilityListener(this);
   origin = target.getAgletInfo().getOrigin();
}

public void onDispatching(MobilityEvent ev) {
   aglet.setText("I'm leaving for " + ev.getLocation());
}

public void onArrival(MobilityEvent ev) {
   if (atOrigin (ev.getLocation()) == false) {
      try {
         target.dispatchnewURL(origin);
      } catch (Exception ex) {}
   }
}

boolean atOrigin(URL current) {
   return origin.equals(current.toString());
}

public void onRetract(MobilityEvent ev) {
}
}
```

3.3.3 The Aglet Communication Model

Aglets communicate by message passing. The messaging facility allows aglets to create and exchange messages in flexible ways (see Figure 3-5). By default, aglet messaging does not assume concurrent message handling. This means that all messages are handled one by one. Please refer to Chapter 6 (Aglet Messaging) for more information on concurrency and more details about aglet messaging.

In addition to Aglet and AgletProxy, the following are key components of the aglet communication model.

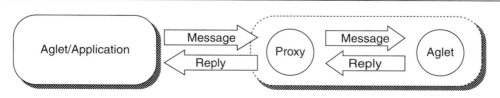

FIGURE 3-5 Aglet-to-Aglet Messaging

- *Message.* A message is an object exchanged between aglets. It allows for synchronous as well as asynchronous message passing between aglets. Message passing can be used by aglets to collaborate and exchange information in a loosely coupled fashion.

- *Future reply.* A future reply is used in asynchronous message sending as a handle that allows the message sender to receive a reply asynchronously.

- *Reply set.* A reply set can contain multiple future reply objects and is used to get results as they become available. With this object, the sender can also choose to get the first result and ignore subsequent replies.

3.4   Aglet Package

Now let's take a quick tour of the core classes and interfaces of the Aglet API, which you will use to create and operate aglets. It contains methods for initializing an aglet and message handling, as well as dispatching, deactivating/activating, retracting, cloning, and disposing of aglets. The Aglet API is simple and flexible. Created in the spirit of Java and representing a lightweight, pragmatic approach to mobile agents, the Aglet API is a Java package (`aglet`) consisting of classes and interfaces, most notably `Aglet`, `AgletProxy`, `AgletContext`, `Message`, `FutureReply`, and `AgletID`. (Actually, the full name of the package includes the name of the manufacturer. In this case, it is `com.ibm.aglet`. For readability we use the short form throughout this book.)

3.4.1   Aglet Class

The `Aglet` class is the key class in the Aglet API. It is the abstract class that you, the aglet developer, use as base class when you create your customized aglets. The `Aglet` class defines methods for controlling its own life cycle: methods for cloning, dispatching, deactivating, and disposing of itself. It also defines methods that are supposed to be overridden in its subclasses by the aglet programmer and provides you with the necessary hooks to customize the aglet's behavior. These methods are systematically invoked by the system when certain events take place in the life cycle of an aglet.

Let us look at some of the methods in the `Aglet` class. The `dispatch` method causes an aglet to move from the local host to the destination given as the argument. The `deactivate` method allows an aglet to be stored in secondary storage, and the `clone` method spawns a new instance of the aglet, which has the state of the original aglet.

The `Aglet` class is also used to access the attributes associated with an aglet. The `AgletInfo` object, which can be obtained by `getAgletInfo()`, contains an aglet's built-in attributes, such as its creation time and code base, as well as its dynamic attributes, such as its arrival time and the address of its current context.

Now let us show you how simple it is to create a customized aglet. Start by importing the aglet package, which contains all the definitions of the Aglet API. Next, define the MyFirstAglet class, which inherits from the Aglet class:

```
import com.ibm.aglet.*;
public class MyFirstAglet extends Aglet {
    // Put aglet's methods here
}
```

For example, if you want your aglet to perform some specific initialization when it is created, you override its onCreation method:

```
public void onCreation(Object init) {
    // Do some initialization here...
}
```

When an aglet has been created or when it arrives in a new context, it is given its own thread of execution through a system invocation of its run method. You can see this invocation as a means of giving the aglet a degree of autonomy. The run method is called every time the aglet arrives at or is activated in a new context. You can say that the run method becomes the main entry point for the aglet's thread of execution. By overriding this method, you can customize your aglet's autonomous behavior.

```
public void run() {
    // Do something else here...
}
```

For example, you can use run() to let the aglet dispatch itself to a remote context. You can do so by letting the aglet call its dispatch method with the uniform resource locator (URL) of the remote host as the argument. This URL should specify the host and domain names of the destination context and the protocol (atp) to be used for transferring the aglet over the network. (ATP is the Agent Transfer Protocol, an HTTP-like protocol developed for mobile Internet agents; see Chapter 9.) The URL can also include the name of the remote context (if more than one context is supported at the remote server). If no context name is specified, the aglet will move into the default context.

```
dispatch(new URL("atp://some.host.com/context"));
```

What exactly happens to your aglet when dispatch() is called? Basically, the aglet will disappear from your machine and will reappear in the same object state at the specified destination. First, a special technique called object serialization is used to preserve the state information of the aglet. It makes a sequential byte representation of the aglet. Next, it is passed to the underlying transfer layer, which brings the aglet (byte code and state information) safely over the network. Finally, the transferred bytes are deserialized to re-create the aglet's state (see Figure 3-6).

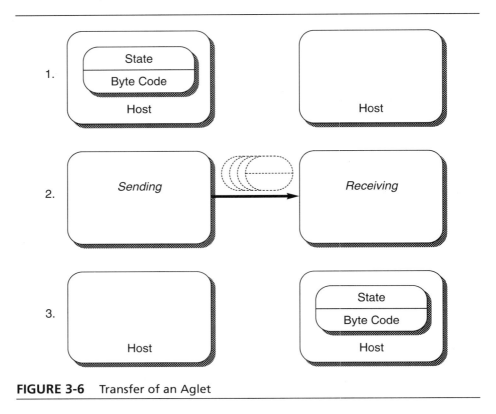

FIGURE 3-6   Transfer of an Aglet

Following this overview of the Aglet class, let us move on to the AgletProxy interface, another core component of the Aglet API.

3.4.2   AgletProxy Interface

The AgletProxy interface acts as the handle of an aglet and provides a common way of accessing the aglet. Because an aglet class has several public methods that should not be accessed directly from other aglets for security reasons, any aglet that wants to communicate with other aglets must first obtain the proxy and then interact through this interface. In other words, the aglet proxy acts as a shield object that protects an aglet from malicious aglets. When invoked, the Aglet-Proxy object consults the *security manager* to determine whether the current execution context is permitted to perform the method. Another important role of the AgletProxy interface is to provide the aglet with location transparency. If the actual aglet resides at a remote host, the proxy forwards the requests to the remote host and returns the result to the local host.

Creating an aglet is one way to get a proxy. The `AgletContext.createAglet` method will return the proxy of the newly created aglet. Other methods that return proxies include `AgletContext.retractAglet`, `AgletProxy.clone`, and `AgletProxy.dispatch`. Note that we use the dot notation (*class.method*) to denote the class that a given method belongs to.

Proxies of existing aglets can also be obtained in the following ways.

- The aglet can get its own proxy by use of `Aglet.getProxy()`.

- You can retrieve an enumeration of proxies in a context by calling the `AgletContext.getAgletProxies` method.

- You can get an aglet proxy for a given aglet identifier via the `AgletContext.getAgletProxy` method.

- You can get an aglet proxy via message passing. An `AgletProxy` object can be put into a `Message` object as an argument and sent to the aglet locally or remotely.

- You can put an `AgletProxy` object into a context property by using the `AgletContext.setProperty` method and share the proxy object.

The `Aglets` framework provides an implementation of the `AgletProxy` interface, so aglet programmers need not implement this interface.

3.4.3   AgletContext Interface

An aglet *context* is the equivalent of a *place*. An aglet spends most of its life in an aglet context. It is created in the context, it goes to sleep there, and it dies there. When it travels in a network, it moves from context to context. In other words, the context is a uniform execution environment for aglets in an otherwise heterogeneous world.

An aglet uses the `AgletContext` interface to get information about its environment and to send messages to the environment, including other aglets currently active in that environment. This interface provides means for maintaining and managing running aglets in an environment where the host system is secured against malicious aglets.

The `Aglet` class has a method for gaining access to its current context:

```
context = getAgletContext();
```

With access to the context, the aglet can create new aglets:

```
context.createAglet(...);
```

And it can retract (pull) remotely located aglets into the current context:

```
context.retractAglet(remoteContextURL, agletID);
```

The aglet can also retrieve a list (enumeration) of proxies of its fellow aglets present in the same context:

```
proxies = context.getAgletProxies();
```

An implementation of this interface is provided by the Aglet package.

3.4.4   Message Class

Aglets communicate by exchanging objects of the Message class. A string field named "kind" distinguishes messages. This field is set when the message is created. The second parameter of the message constructor is an optional message argument:

```
Message myName = new Message("my name", "Jacob");
Message yourName = new Message("your name?");
```

Having created the message objects, we can send them to an aglet by invoking one of the following methods defined in the AgletProxy class:

- Object sendMessage(Message msg)
- FutureReply sendFutureMessage(Message msg)
- void sendOnewayMessage(Message msg)

The Message object is passed as an argument to the aglet's handleMessage method. It is now up to this method to handle the incoming messages. It should return true if a given message is handled; otherwise, it should return false. The sender will then know whether the aglet actually handled the message. In this example, the aglet will recognize and respond accordingly to "hello" messages:

```
public boolean handleMessage(Message msg) {
    if (msg.sameKind("hello")) {
      doHello();    // Respond to the 'hello' message...
      return true;  // Yes, I handled this message.
    } else
      return false; // No, I did not handle this message.
}
```

Only from yourName do we expect to receive a return value:

```
proxy.sendMessage(myName);
String name = (String)proxy.sendMessage(yourName);
```

In the aglet's handleMessage method, we distinguish between the myName message and the yourName message by testing the "kind" field of incoming messages. From myName we extract the name argument, and for yourName we set the return value (sendReply()):

```
public boolean handleMessage(Message msg) {
    if (msg.somekind("my name")) {
       String name = (String)msg.getArg();  // Gets the name...
       return true;   // Yes, I handled this message.
    } else if (msg.somekind("your name?")) {
```

```
        msg.sendReply("Yina");              // Returns its name...
        return true;  // Yes, I handled this message.
    } else
        return false; // No, I did not handle this message.
}
```

3.4.5 FutureReply Class

The object defined by the FutureReply interface is returned by the asynchronous message-sending method and is used as a handle to later receive the result asynchronously. With this interface, the receiver can determine whether a reply is available and can wait for the result with a specified time-out value so that it can continue its execution if a reply was not returned within the specified time. In this example the sender of a message can perform another task (doPeriodicWork()) while waiting for the reply.

```
FutureReply future = proxy.sendFutureMessage(msg);
while (!future.isAvailable()) {
    doPeriodicWork();
}
Object reply = future.getReply();
```

3.4.6 AgletID Class

Every aglet is assigned a globally unique identity that it keeps throughout its lifetime. The AgletID class is a convenient abstraction for this identity. The identifier object hides the implementation-specific representation of the aglet identity. The identifier is an immutable object that you can retrieve directly from the aglet and its proxy:

```
AgletID aid = proxy.getAgletID();
```

Having the identifier and a context, you can always query the context to retrieve the aglet with that identity:

```
proxy = context.getAgletProxy(aid);
```

3.5 Aglet Example: Remote File Update

Let us conclude this chapter with an annotated example of an aglet that updates files by replacing all occurrences of one specified word in the files with another specified word.

The philosophy behind this aglet is the following. For files larger than a certain size it is considered beneficial (it saves network bandwidth) to perform a distributed update of the files, because it saves downloading and uploading of the file and distributes the load of the update to multiple servers (see Figure 3-7).

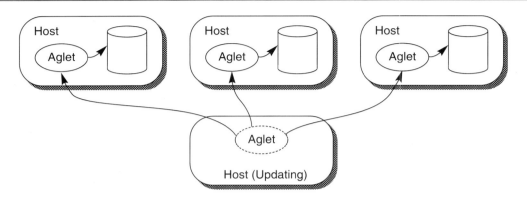

FIGURE 3-7   Multiple Aglets Updating Files in Parallel

To update multiple remotely located files in parallel, we have created the
UpdateFile aglet. Here is the full source code for this aglet:

```
 1: import com.ibm.aglet.*;
 2: import com.ibm.aglet.event.*;
 3: import java.net.*;
 4: import java.io.*;
 5: public class UpdateFile extends Aglet {
 6:     URL destination = null;
 7:     File dir = null;
 8:     String from = null;
 9:     String to = null;
10:     public void onCreation(Object args) {
11:         destination = (URL)((Object[])args)[0];
12:         dir = (File)((Object[])args)[1];
13:         from = (String)((Object[])args)[2];
14:         to = (String)((Object[])args)[3];
15:         addMobilityListener(
16:             new MobilityAdapter() {
17:                 public void onArrival(MobilityEvent e) {
18:                     replace(args.file, args.from, args.to);
19:                     dispose();
20:                 }
21:             }
22:         );
23:         try {
24:             dispatch(args.destination);
25:         } catch (Exception e) {
26:             System.out.println("Failed to dispatch.");
27:         }
28:     }
```

```
29:     void replace(File file, String from, String to) {
30:         // Open 'file' and replace 'from' with 'to'.
31:     }
32: }
```

Let's walk through the source code line by line to give you an idea of what a real aglet looks like. Lines 1 through 4 import the necessary `aglet` and `java` packages. Line 5 defines the public `UpdateFile` class as an extension of the `Aglet` class. Line 6 defines a field that stores the initialization arguments (`args`). Lines 10 through 28 define the aglet's `onCreation` method, which is invoked by the system when the aglet is created. The parameter, `args`, contains the initialization arguments for the aglet. In lines 11 through 14 they are stored in their respective fields. Line 15 adds a mobility listener object to the aglet. This object and its class are first defined as an inner class and then instantiated in lines 16 through 21. This listener defines one handler method (`onArrival`). This method will automatically be invoked by the system when the aglet arrives at a new host. Line 18 invokes the method that will update the file (defined in lines 29 through 31). Line 19 ensures that the aglet will dispose of itself when it has completed the file update. The remaining part of the `onCreation` method, lines 23 through 27, will manage the dispatch (line 24) of the aglet to its destination.

As soon as the `UpdateFile` aglet is created it will (1) instantiate its mobility listener, (2) add the listener to its event-handling mechanism, and (3) dispatch itself to the destination host. When it arrives at the destination host, the `onArrival` method will perform the file update, followed by disposal of the aglet.

Now let us present the code fragment needed to initialize the argument object and create the `UpdateFile` aglet. This code fragment is taken from a stationary aglet that remains on the updating host while the `UpdateFile` aglets move to their respective hosts. Lines 1 through 5 initialize the argument object, `args`, with destination URL, file path, matching word, and replacement word. In line 6, we first get a reference to the aglet context. The context is used in line 7 to create the aglet named `UpdateFile` with the arguments in `args`. The context is needed because aglets cannot exist in a vacuum. They require the context for proper creation and execution.

```
1: Object args = new Object[] {
2:     new URL("atp://java.trl.ibm.co.jp"),
3:     new File("C:/public/test.dat"),
4:     "abc",
5:     "xyz" };
6: AgletContext context = getAgletContext()
7: context.createAglet(null, "UpdateFile", args);
```

3.6 Summary

As discussed in this chapter, we have found Java to be an excellent vehicle for mobile agents. Many of Java's characteristics are valuable for mobile agent systems. The most important ones are platform independence, secure execution, dynamic class loading, multithread programming, object serialization, and introspection. We also outlined significant shortcomings. The most significant of these are inadequate support for resource control, lack of protection of references, lack of object ownership of references, and lack of support for preservation and resumption of the execution state. Some of these shortcomings can be worked around; others are more serious and have implications for the overall conceptual design and deployment of Java-based mobile agent systems.

We also introduced the aglet object model. This model was designed to benefit from the agent characteristics of Java while overcoming some of the deficiencies in the language system. In the aglet object model, a mobile agent has its own thread of control, is event-driven, and communicates by message passing. An aglet is autonomous, because it runs in its own thread of execution after arriving at a host, and it is reactive, because it can respond to incoming messages. Some of the other basic elements of the aglet model are the proxy, context, message, future reply, and identifier. The aglet object model also defines an event model with three predefined event handlers (listeners): clone listener, mobility listener, and persistence listener.

Chapter 4 examines the anatomy of an aglet in greater detail. It explains the overridable methods and the role they play in the events of an aglet's lifetime.

Chapter 4
Anatomy of an Aglet

After reading this chapter you should have a basic understanding of the anatomy of an aglet. You will learn about the methods in the aglet that can be overridden by the programmer. These methods are systematically invoked by the system as important events in the life of an aglet. We will show you the principles for using these methods, including important information about the order in which they are invoked by the system when specific events take place. With this knowledge, you should be in position to create aglets that can perform simple tasks on remote computers.

Let us use the aglet's life cycle as a starting point for this chapter. What can happen to an aglet during its lifetime? Many things—but first it must be created. An aglet can be created as an instance of an aglet class; this is the normal way to create an object in a programming language such as Java. Another way to create an aglet is by *cloning* an existing aglet; this will result in the creation of a twin aglet.

Now that one or more aglets exist, we can send, or dispatch, them on a trip to a remote site. Having dispatched an aglet, we can wait for it to come back or we can force it back by *retracting* it. When the aglet has safely returned home we can store it on a hard disk for later use, in which case we say that we have *deactivated* the aglet. Later, we can wake it up by *activating* it. If the aglet is no longer of use we can simply choose to *dispose* of it.

The main events in the life of an aglet can thus be categorized as follows:

- *Creation*—create or clone
- *Disposal*—dispose
- *Mobility*—dispatch and retract
- *Persistence*—deactivate and activate

4.1   Creation

To do anything with an aglet you must first create it by instantiating it from an aglet class or cloning an existing aglet. We will describe both ways, starting with class instantiation.

The aglet is created in a context, where it will spend most of its life. When it moves from machine to machine, it moves from context to context. You can regard a context as a uniform environment for the aglet. Whether the aglet is executing on a PC with Windows or on a UNIX workstation, it is guaranteed a fixed set of services from the context. One of these services, which we will demonstrate, is instantiation of new aglets from a given aglet class. For an aglet to instantiate new aglets it needs access to its current context. It can gain this access by calling the getAgletContext method in its own interface.

```
public final AgletContext Aglet.getAgletContext()
```
Gets the context in which the aglet is currently executing.

For example, if an aglet executing in a given context wished to create an instance of the SomeAglet class located on the same code base in the same context, it would first have to get the current context and then invoke the createAglet method in that context. The resulting aglet program line would look something like this:

```
getAgletContext().createAglet(getCodeBase(), "SomeAglet", null);
```

The createAglet method has three arguments. The first argument, which defines the code base of the aglet, is a URL; the second is the name of the aglet class; and the third consists of a possible initialization argument for the coming aglet. For a full description of the createAglet method, see Chapter 5.

Do not attempt to instantiate an aglet directly from its constructor by using the new statement in Java. All aglet instances must be properly initialized after instantiation. Otherwise, their behavior will be largely unpredictable.

Although the aglet context will control the creation of the new aglet, this does not mean that you as an aglet programmer have no influence over it. There are several hooks that you can use to customize the behavior of the aglet during its creation. In fact, these hooks are methods that you can override in the aglet subclass to implement the desired behavior. Three methods are of particular interest here: the aglet's constructor, onCreation(), and run().

protected **Aglet.Aglet()**

Constructs an uninitialized aglet. This method is called only once in the life cycle of an aglet. As a rule, you should generally avoid overriding this constructor. Instead, you should override onCreation() to initialize the aglet upon creation.

Public void **Aglet.onCreation(Object init)**

Initializes the new aglet. This method is called only once in the life cycle of an aglet. Override this method for custom initialization of the aglet.

Public void **Aglet.run()**

The entry point for the aglet's own thread of execution. This method is invoked upon a successful creation, dispatch, retraction, or activation of the aglet.

These methods are automatically invoked by the context during the creation of the aglet. Two of them—onCreation and run—provide you with an elegant way of customizing the aglet creation. However, to take full advantage of this mechanism, you must understand how these methods collaborate. We will use *method collaboration diagrams* to illustrate this concept.

First, the createAglet method in the aglet context is called. The topmost horizontal bar in Figure 4-1 represents its execution. During the execution, createAglet() will create an instance of the given aglet class, which is seen as an invocation of the aglet's constructor (Aglet()). Generally, horizontal bars represent the execution of the aglet code. When the aglet instance has been constructed, onCreation() is invoked, and when that has been executed, run() is invoked. The execution of onCreation() and run() takes place in different threads from the original thread of createAglet(), and execution of onCreation() is guaranteed to finish before that of run() starts.

In the following example, we let the aglet, CreationExample, create an instance of the aglet class named CreationChild. CreationExample extends the Aglet class:

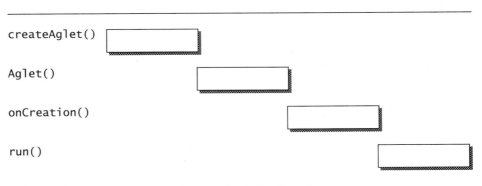

createAglet()

Aglet()

onCreation()

run()

FIGURE 4-1   Collaboration Diagram for Aglet Creation

```
public class CreationExample extends Aglet {
   public void run() {
      try {
         getAgletContext().createAglet(
            getCodeBase(), "CreationChild", null)
         );
      } catch (Exception e) {
         System.out.println(e.getMessage());
      }
   }
}
```

The only method that this aglet implements is its run method, which calls for the aglet's own context to create an aglet of the CreationChild class. Notice that the program catches any exception thrown during the creation of the aglet and prints the error message. CreationChild itself extends the Aglet class and overrides three methods: the constructor, onCreation(), and run(). The systematic invocation of these methods is demonstrated by the console output they generate.

```
public class CreationChild extends Aglet {
   public CreationChild() {
      // Print to the console...
   }

   public void onCreation(Object init) {
      // Print to the console...
   }

   public void run() {
      // Print to the console...
   }
}
```

4.2 Aglet Disposal

The aglet takes up various resources while it is in an aglet context. It is therefore good aglet ethics to properly dispose of the aglet after it has fulfilled its task. Remember that most aglets will perform their tasks at remote servers as *guests*, and as such they are obliged to minimize their consumption of the host's resources.

The system will reclaim all threads belonging to an aglet that is disposed of. In addition, the aglet context will release all of its resources that are tied to that aglet. In doing so, it will eliminate all references between the context and the aglet to be disposed of. However, there is no guarantee that the memory allocated by the aglet will be deallocated immediately. The Java garbage collector will clear away the aglet when all references to it have been eliminated, including references from other aglets.

For the aglet to dispose of itself, it should invoke its dispose method. Notice that this method is final, which means that you cannot override it and change its meaning.

public final void **Aglet.dispose()**

Destroys and removes the aglet from its current aglet context. A successful invocation of this method will kill all threads created by the given aglet.

A call to dispose() will immediately lead to invocation of the onDisposing method, which is your hook for customizing the disposal process. You can override this method with any actions that should precede the actual disposal of the aglet. For example, you may use the method to allow the aglet to prepare for its own disposal by closing associated files and windows. It is important that the aglet release all resources before it is disposed of. For example, if the aglet has created a window, the window would be left behind if the aglet gets disposed of without explicitly closing the window.

public void **Aglet.onDisposing()**

Called when an attempt is made to dispose of the aglet. Subclasses can override this method to implement actions that should be taken in response to a request for disposal.

The method collaboration diagram shown in Figure 4-2 illustrates what happens when the aglet disposes of itself. In an aglet's thread of execution, which may be simultaneous to the execution of its run method, it invokes the dispose method, which in turn invokes the onDisposing method. On the completion of the latter, all threads created by the given aglet are killed. This includes the initial call to dispose() as long as it is executed by one of the aglet's own threads.

DisposalExample is an example of an aglet that disposes of itself immediately after it has been created. As soon as the aglet is created and its run method is called, it invokes dispose(). The onDisposing method is called, and the aglet disappears.

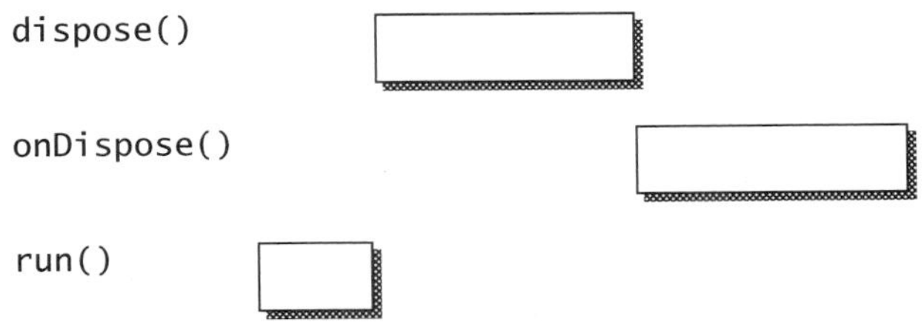

dispose()

onDispose()

run()

FIGURE 4-2   Collaboration Diagram for Aglet Disposal

```
public class DisposalExample extends Aglet {

    public void onDisposing() {
        // Print to the console...
    }

    public void run() {
        dispose();
        // You should never get here!
    }
}
```

4.3　Delegation-Based Event Model

A delegation-based event model provides uniform handling of aglet cloning, mobility, and persistence. When an aglet is cloned, moved, or saved to secondary storage it will result in a number of *events* being sent to the aglet. The different event types are encapsulated in a class hierarchy in the `com.ibm.aglet.event` package. An event is propagated from the agent system to an aglet's listener object by invoking a method on the listener and passing the instance of the event subclass that defines the event type generated. Three types of event are defined:

CloneEvent

MobilityEvent

PersistencyEvent

A listener is an object that implements a specific listener interface. These interfaces define one or more methods that are to be invoked by the event source in response to each specific event type handled by the interface.

A listener interface will typically have a separate method for each distinct event type the event class represents. In essence, particular event semantics are defined by the combination of an `AgletEvent` class paired with a particular method in a listener interface. For example, the `CloneListener` interface defines three methods—onCloning, onClone, and onCloned—one for each event type that `CloneEvent` class represents. Three listener interfaces are defined:

CloneListener

MobilityListener

PersistencyListener

The aglet event API attempts to strike a balance between, on the one hand, providing a reasonable granularity of listener interface types and, on the other hand, providing a separate interface for every single event type. The listener interfaces are accompanied by a set of abstract *adapter* classes that implements each listener interface. These classes allow programmers to easily subclass the adapters and override *only* the listener methods they are interested in. The `Adapter` classes provided by the event API are as follows:

`CloneAdapter`

`MobilityAdapter`

`PersistencyAdapter`

In the following sections we will describe how each of the adapter classes is used to handle aglet cloning, mobility, and persistence.

4.4 Cloning

Let us start with cloning, an alternative way of creating new aglets. If you already have an aglet in your context, you can create its twin by using the aglet's `clone` method. A successful invocation of this method on a given aglet will create an identical copy (clone) of it in the current aglet context. Note that this method does not return the clone directly but instead returns the aglet's proxy to you. The proxy is a placeholder for the aglet, serving to shield it from direct access to its public methods. You will hear more about the aglet proxy later.

public final Object **Aglet.clone()**

Clones the aglet. Notice that it is the proxy for the cloned aglet that is returned by this method.

The aglet delegation-based event model provides you with a simple and efficient scheme to customize and control the cloning process. Listeners are added to the aglet and are removed from it by two methods: `addCloneListener` and `removeCloneListener`.

public final void **Aglet.addCloneListener(CloneListener listener)**

Adds the specified clone listener to receive clone events.

public final void **Aglet.removeCloneListener(CloneListener listener)**

Removes the specified clone listener so that it no longer receives clone events.

Three methods in the clone listener allow you to customize and control the cloning process. The first, `onCloning`, is called in the aglet that you attempt to clone. To disable cloning, you can simply override this method to throw a `SecurityException`. The second method, `onClone`, can be used to initialize the clone. The third method, `onCloned`, is invoked in the original after the cloning has taken place.

public **CloneAdapter.CloneAdapter ()**

Creates an instance of the clone adapter.

public void **CloneAdapter.onCloning(CloneEvent event)**

Called when you attempt to clone an aglet. Subclasses can override this method to implement any actions that should be taken in response to a cloning request.

public void **CloneAdapter.onClone(CloneEvent event)**

Initializes the cloned aglet. Override this method for custom initialization of the cloned aglet.

public void **CloneAdapter.onCloned(CloneEvent event)**

Called in the original aglet when the cloning has taken place.

How do these methods collaborate? Let the bars above the dotted line in Figure 4-3 represent execution in the aglet that is being cloned, and let the lower bars represent the resulting aglet clone. Initially, the aglet's clone method is called. The topmost horizontal bar represents the execution of this method. The clone method will invoke the onCloning method in the clone adapter of the aglet that is to be cloned. On completion of this method, clone() will resume execution and create the twin aglet. The very first method to be invoked in a separate thread of execution in this new aglet will be the onClone method in its clone adapter, followed by the run method. Simultaneously, the invocation of the onCloned method in the first aglet indicates that the cloning has taken place.

In this example we let the CloningExample aglet clone itself. CloningExample extends the Aglet class and overrides two methods: onCreation and run. The onCreation method is used to install a clone event listener in the aglet. The listener is defined as an *inner class* that extends the CloneAdapter class. Inner classes allow classes to be defined in any scope. You can now define inner classes

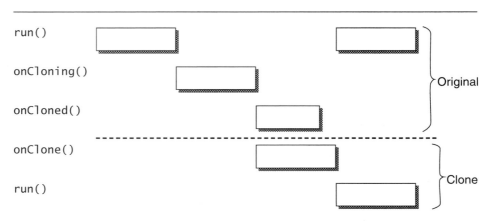

FIGURE 4-3   Collaboration Diagram for Aglet Cloning

as members of other classes, locally within a block of statements, or (anonymously) within an expression.

Notice that we have added to the class a Boolean field, _theClone. This field is used to distinguish between the parent aglet and its cloned twin. It works as follows. Initially, the value of the field is set to false. When the aglet is cloned, the clone will inherit this field and its value, which remains false. Because we are guaranteed that onClone() will be invoked only in the clone *and* that this will occur before run() is invoked, we can safely let the onClone method toggle the value of the _theClone field. In the run method it is now safe to use the _theClone field to prevent the clone from starting to clone.

```
public class CloningExample extends Aglet {

    boolean _theClone = false;

    public void onCreation(Object o) {
        addCloneListener(
          new CloneAdapter() {
            public void onCloning(CloneEvent e) {
                // Print to the console...
            }
            public void onClone(CloneEvent e) {
                _theClone = true;   //- Yes, I am the clone.
                // Print to the console...
            }
            public void onCloned(CloneEvent e) {
                // Print to the console...
            }
          }
        );
    }

    public void run() {
    if (!_theClone) {
       // The parent runs here...
       try {
          clone();
       } catch (Exception e) {
          System.out.println(e.getMessage());
       }
    } else {
       // The clone runs here...
    }
    }
}
```

4.5   Aglet Mobility

There are two ways to move an aglet. One is to dispatch (*push*) it to a remote location. More specifically, dispatching the aglet means requesting it to go to another location to continue its execution there. The other way to move an aglet is to retract (*pull*) it from a remote context. By retracting the aglet, we are requesting it to return from a remote location. Retraction often follows a previous dispatch of the aglet to the given remote context.

4.5.1 Dispatching

The `dispatch` method and the uniform resource locator are your tools for requesting an aglet to visit a remote machine. Like the `dispose` method, `dispatch()` cannot be overridden.

> `public final void` **`Aglet.dispatch(URL destination)`**
>
> Dispatches the aglet to the location (context) specified by the destination argument.

The URL is a standard way of specifying the location of a resource on the Internet. In addition to host and domain names, the URL includes information about the protocol to be used for communicating with the remote server. The Aglets framework uses `atp` (Agent Transfer Protocol) as a network protocol for dispatching aglets. The `dispatch` method does not force you to use a specific protocol. Your choice of protocol depends entirely on the set of protocols supported by the implementation of the Aglet API that you are using *and* of the protocols supported by the remote server. The following program line is an example of a dispatch call with an associated URL using the `atp` protocol to dispatch the aglet to the default context in a server at `some.host.com`:

```
dispatch(new URL("atp://some.host.com"));
```

The URL can also include the name of the remote context (if more than one context is supported at the remote server). In the following example we dispatch the aglet to the `public` context at the remote server at `some.host.com`:

```
dispatch(new URL("atp://some.host.com/public"));
```

The aglet delegation-based event model also provides you with a simple and efficient scheme to control the dispatching process. Listeners are added to and removed from the aglet by the two methods `addMobilityListener` and `removeMobilityListener`.

> `public final void` **`Aglet.addMobilityListener(MobilityListener listener)`**
>
> Adds the specified mobility listener to receive mobility events.

> `public final void` **`Aglet.removeMobilityListener(MobilityListener listener)`**
>
> Removes the specified mobility listener so that it no longer receives mobility events.

Calling `dispatch()` on an aglet will immediately lead to the invocation of the listener's `onDispatching` method. This method is a hook that allows you to customize dispatching. You can override it to allow the aglet to finish its current task and prepare it for the trip to its next destination. Upon successful invocation of dispatch(), the listener's onArrival method is called, followed by the invocation of the aglet's run(). The onArrival method can be used to initialize the aglet once it has arrived at the new destination.

public **MobilityAdapter.MobilityAdapter ()**

Creates an instance of the mobility adapter.

public void **MobilityAdapter.onDispatching(MobilityEvent event)**

Called when an attempt is made to dispatch the aglet. Subclasses can override this method to implement actions that should be taken in response to a dispatch request.

public void **MobilityAdapter.onArrival(MobilityEvent event)**

Initializes the newly arrived aglet. Subclasses can override this method to implement actions that should be taken on arrival of the aglet at a new host.

Figure 4-4 illustrates how a set of dispatch-related methods collaborates. The bars above the dotted line represent the aglet's execution before it is dispatched, and the lower bars represent its execution at its destination. In an aglet's thread of execution, which may be simultaneous to the execution of its run method, it invokes the dispatch method, which in turn invokes the listener's onDispatching method. On completion of the latter method, all threads created by the aglet are killed and the aglet is transferred to its destination. The first method to be invoked at the destination is the listener's onArrival method, followed by the run method.

In this example we let the DispatchingExample aglet dispatch itself. The example is based on the same template as the previous cloning example. Dis-

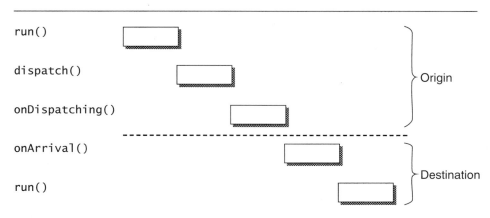

FIGURE 4-4   Collaboration Diagram for Aglet Dispatch

patchingExample extends the Aglet class and overrides two methods: onCreation and run. The listener is defined as an inner class that extends the MobilityAdapter class. Again we use a Boolean field, _theRemote, to distinguish between the aglet before and after it has been dispatched. When this aglet is created and starts running (run()), it creates a URL for its destination. For simplicity, we let that destination be the current host. When the aglet has been dispatched, all its threads will be killed. In other words, you should not expect the execution to return from a successful call to the dispatch method. When the aglet arrives at a new host, onArrival is called and the Boolean field is toggled. The aglet will now remain at this host until it is disposed of.

```
public class DispatchingExample extends Aglet {

    boolean _theRemote = false;

    public void onCreation(Object init) {
        addMobilityListener(
            new MobilityAdapter() {
                public void onDispatching(MobilityEvent e) {
                    // Print to the console...
                }
                public void onArrival(MobilityEvent e) {
                    _theRemote = true;  //- Yes, I am the remote aglet.
                    // Print to the console...
                }
            }
        );
    }

    public void run() {
        if (!_theRemote) {
            // The original aglet runs here
            try {
                URL destination = new URL((String)getAgletContext().
                                         getProperty("location"));
                dispatch(destination);
                // You should never get here!
            } catch (Exception e) {
                System.out.println(e.getMessage());
            }
        } else {
            // The remote aglet runs here...
        }
    }
}
```

4.5.2   Retracting

Sometimes you may not want to wait for an aglet to return on its own but instead may prefer to pull it back, perhaps in an asynchronous fashion. The retract-

Aglet method in the aglet context allows you to do this. The method takes two arguments that specify the remote host as well as the specific aglet to be retracted:

```
AgletContext.retractAglet(URL contextAddress, AgletID aid)
```

An aglet is associated with a unique identifier so that every aglet in the network can be uniquely addressed by combining its identifier with its context URL. You will hear more about the context's retractAglet method and aglet identifiers in a later chapter.

The mobility listener supports two methods to handle retraction: onArrival(), which we have already explained, and the onReverting method. An attempt to retract a remote aglet will lead to the invocation of onReverting(). This method invocation can be used as a warning that someone is attempting to retract the aglet. Override this method to allow the aglet to prepare for retraction. The method can also be used to prevent retraction.

Public void **MobilityAdapter.onReverting(MobilityEvent event)**

Called when someone from a remote location attempts to retract the aglet. Subclasses can override this method to implement actions that should be taken in response to a request for retraction.

Let us see how the methods related to retraction collaborate when the retractAglet method in the local aglet context is called. The topmost horizontal bar in Figure 4-5 represents its execution. The two bars below the dotted line represent the execution threads of the remote aglet. The invocation of retractAglet() leads to remote invocation of onReverting(). All threads of the remote aglet are killed upon successful completion of the onReverting method. The two bars immediately above the dotted line show the execution threads of the aglet

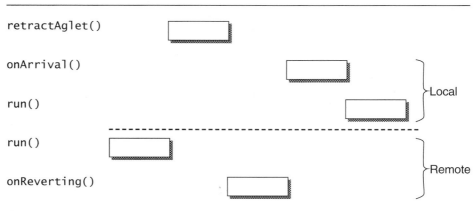

FIGURE 4-5   Collaboration Diagram for Aglet Retraction

after its return. Execution of the onArrival method is guaranteed to finish before run() starts.

This example demonstrates how an aglet, RetractionExample, can retract an aglet, RetractionChild, that it has previously dispatched to an aglet server.

```
public class RetractionExample extends Aglet {

    public void run() {
        try {
            AgletProxy proxy = getAgletContext().createAglet(null,
                "RetractionChild",null);
            URL destination = new URL(atp://some.host.com);
            AgletID aid = proxy.getAgletID();
            proxy.dispatch(destination);
            getAgletContext().retractAglet(destination, aid);
        } catch (Exception e) {
            System.out.println(e.getMessage());
        }
    }
}
```

Here you will notice a number of classes and methods that have not yet been introduced, but do not let them confuse you. We will take the body of run() line by line.

In the first line, we use the aglet context to create an instance of the RetractionChild aglet. Creating an aglet in the context returns a reference to a proxy for the new aglet. Later we will use the proxy to dispatch this aglet. In the second line, we retrieve the URL of a remote aglet server. We will use this URL as the destination for the aglet and later as the location from which we retract it. In the next line we retrieve the identity of the aglet, which we need to identify the aglet on the remote server. In line four the proxy is used to dispatch the aglet. Finally, in the fifth line of run(), we use the identity of the remote aglet to retract it from its remote host.

The RetractionChild aglet follows a well-known scheme. It extends the Aglet class and overrides two methods: onCreation and run. The onCreation method installs the mobility listener. Two Boolean variables are introduced to capture the state of the aglet. The _dispatched variable is set in onArrival() when the aglet arrives at the remote host, and _reverted is set in onReverting() when the aglet is about to be retracted. In this example we use these variables to control the console messages printed by the aglet:

```
public class RetractionChild extends Aglet {

    boolean _reverted = false;
    boolean _dispatched = false;

    public void onCreation(Object init) {
        addMobilityListener(
            new MobilityAdapter() {
```

```
                    public void onReverting(MobilityEvent e) {
                        _reverted = true;
                        // Print to the console...
                    }
                    public void onArrival(MobilityEvent e) {
                        _dispatched = true;
                        if (_reverted)
                            // Print to the console...
                    }
                }
            );
        }

    public void run() {
        if (_dispatched)
            // Print to the console...
    }
}
```

4.6 Persistence

The aglet allows you to temporarily store it in secondary storage (see Figure 4-6). To *deactivate* the aglet means to request it to enter a dormant state. The aglet does not actually leave the context, although it does not run any longer. When the aglet returns from its dormant state we say that it has been *activated*.

When you deactivate an aglet you must specify the length of time it should stay deactivated. Notice that the period you specify is only a suggestion to the

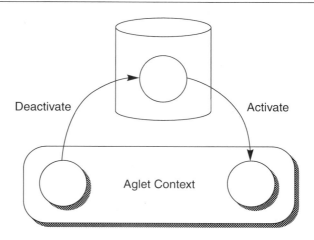

FIGURE 4-6 Aglet Deactivation and Activation

system. The actual time that the aglet is activated depends very much on the implementation you are using and the load on your system.

`public final void` **`deactivate(long duration)`**

Deactivates the aglet. The aglet will temporarily be stopped in its current context. It will resume execution after the specified period has elapsed.

The persistency listener helps you to control the activation and deactivation process of the aglet. Listeners are added to and removed from the aglet by the two methods addPersistencyListener and removePersistencyListener.

`public final void` **`Aglet.addPersistencyListener(Persistency-`**
`Listener listener)`

Adds the specified persistency listener to receive mobility events.

`public final void` **`Aglet.removePersistencyListener(Persistency-`**
`Listener listener)`

Removes the specified persistency listener so that it no longer receives mobility events.

When `deactivate()` is called it will immediately invoke the listener's on-Deactivating method. You should override this method to allow the aglet to finish its current task before going to sleep. The duration of the aglet's sleep is given in milliseconds by the `duration` argument. The aglet will be activated after the specified period has elapsed. The listener's onActivation method can be used to reinitialize the aglet when it is activated. If the specified duration is zero (0), the aglet will deactivate and remain dormant until the aglet server is rebooted. This mechanism is typically used to allow aglets to survive rebooting.

`public` **`PersistencyAdapter.PersistencyAdapter ()`**

Creates an instance of the persistency adapter.

`public void` **`PersistencyAdapter.onDeactivating(PersistencyEvent`**
`event)`

Called when an attempt is made to deactivate the aglet. Subclasses can override this method to implement actions that should be taken in response to a request for deactivation.

`public void` **`PersistencyAdapter.onActivation(PersistencyEvent`**
`event)`

Initializes the newly activated aglet. Subclasses can override this method to implement actions that should be taken on activation of the aglet.

Figure 4-7 illustrates how the set of methods related to deactivation and activation collaborate. The bars above the dotted line represent the aglet's execution before it is deactivated, and the lower bars represent its execution after it is activated. In an aglet's thread of execution, which may be simultaneous with the exe-

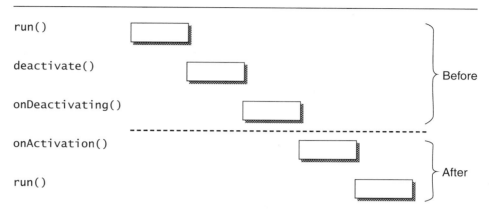

run()

deactivate()

onDeactivating()

— —

onActivation()

run()

Before

After

FIGURE 4-7   Collaboration Diagram for Aglet Deactivation and Activation

cution of its run method, it invokes the deactivate method, which in turn invokes the onDeactivating method. On completion of the latter method, all threads created by the given aglet are killed and the aglet goes to sleep. The first method to be invoked at the destination is the onActivation method, followed by the run method.

Now let us look at an example. The DeactivationExample aglet will deactivate itself for about 10 seconds. DeactivationExample extends the Aglet class and overrides two methods: onCreation and run. As in previous examples in this chapter, we use an inner class to define a listener and a Boolean field, _activated, to distinguish between the aglet before and after it is activated. When this aglet is created and starts running (run()), it immediately deactivates itself. When this happens, all its threads are killed. In other words, you should not expect the execution to return from a successful call to the deactivate method. The aglet context will automatically wake it up when the 10 seconds have elapsed. When the aglet is activated, the onActivation method is called and the Boolean field is toggled. The aglet will now remain at this host until it is disposed of.

```
public class DeactivationExample extends Aglet {

    private static long SECOND = 1000;
    boolean _activated = false;

    public void onCreation(Object init) {
        addPersistencyListener(
            new PersistencyAdapter() {
                public void onDeactivating(PersistencyEvent e) {
                    // Print to the console...
                }
```

```
                    public void onActivation(PersistencyEvent e) {
                        _activated = true;   //- Yes, I am the activated
                                                            aglet.
                        // Print to the console...
                    }
                }
            );
        }

        public void run() {
            if (!_activated) {
                // The original aglet runs here...
                try {
                    deactivate(10 * SECOND);
                    // You should never get here!
                } catch (Exception e) {
                    System.out.println(e.getMessage());
                }
            } else {
                // The activated aglet runs here...
            }
        }
    }
```

4.7   Events

You may have noticed that most of the listener and adapter methods have one argument, an event. We have not yet told you much about these events. There are three kinds of them: CloneEvent, MobilityEvent, and PersistencyEvent. These event objects carry additional information about the specific event that may be useful for the aglet. Let us start with a brief look at CloneEvent.

4.7.1   CloneEvent

This kind of event is received by the following methods in CloneAdapter: onCloning(), onClone(), and onCloned(). CloneEvent has a method, getAglet-Proxy, that retrieves the proxy of the aglet that is being cloned.

Public AgletProxy **CloneEvent.getAgletProxy()**
Returns the aglet proxy of the aglet that is being cloned.

The event object and the getAgletProxy method identify the aglet that is being cloned.

```
public void onCloning(CloneEvent e) {
    try {
        // Print the identity of the aglet that is being cloned.
        print(e.getAgletProxy().getAgletID().toString());
```

```
            } catch (InvalidAgletException iae) {
               // The retrieved aglet is invalid.
            }
      }
```

4.7.2 MobilityEvent

The MobilityEvent object is received by the following methods in Mobility-Adapter: onDispatching(), onArrival(), and onReverting(). As with Clone-Event, the MobilityEvent class supports the getAgletProxy method, which in this case retrieves the proxy of the aglet that is being either dispatched or retracted. The event class also features another method, getLocation. This method allows the aglet to determine the destination of a dispatch or retract request.

Public AgletProxy **MobilityEvent.getAgletProxy()**

Returns the aglet proxy of the aglet that is being dispatched.

Public URL **MobilityEvent.getLocation()**

Gets the location. This specifies the destination of a dispatch if the mobility event is *dispatching*. It specifies the requester of a retraction if the event is *reverting*. Finally, it specifies the host at which it arrived if the event has *arrived*.

Let us show you how an aglet can use getLocation() in the adapter's onDispatching method to determine the URL of the server that it is about to visit. This information may enable the aglet to control where it is sent to.

```
public void onDispatching(MobilityEvent e) {
      // Print where you are going to.
      print(e.getLocation().toString());
}
```

4.7.3 PersistencyEvent

The last kind of aglet event is PersistencyEvent, which is received by onDeactivating() and onActivation() in the PersistencyAdapter. Use getAgletProxy() to find out who is deactivating a given aglet, and use getDuration() to let the aglet know the length of time it will remain deactivated.

Public AgletProxy **PersistencyAdapter.getAgletProxy()**

Returns the aglet proxy that is being activated or deactivated.

Public long **PersistencyAdapter.getDuration()**

Gets the duration in milliseconds.

The getDuration method prints the time (in milliseconds) that the aglet will be deactivated.

```
public void onDeactivating(PersistencyEvent e) {
    // Print how long you are going to be deactivated.
    print(e.getDuration());
}
```

4.8 Aglet Example: Directory Listing

Let us conclude this chapter with a practical aglet that can be sent out to capture a directory listing on a remote host and then returns by itself to the origin to display the listing (see Figure 4-8). ListingAglet has four instance variables: back, which is a Boolean variable that becomes true when the aglet is about to return to its origin; dir, which contains path information for the directory listing; list, which contains the result of the directory listing; and origin, which is the URL of the origin of the aglet.

The aglet implements the onCreation method, which installs a mobility listener that handles the mobility event. When the aglet arrives at the remote host, back is false; assuming that the aglet is given the proper security permissions, it will capture the local directory listing in list. When that listing has been completed, back is set to true. When the aglet returns to its origin, it will display the directory listing.

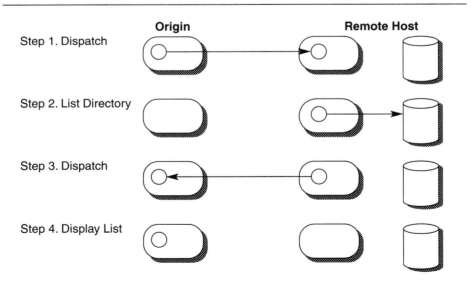

FIGURE 4-8   Directory Listing Aglet

```
public class ListingAglet extends Aglet {
    boolean back = false;
    File dir = new File("C:/PUBLIC");
    String[] list;
    URL origin = null;

    public void onCreation(Object o) {
        addMobilityListener(
            new MobilityAdapter() {
                public void onArrival(MobilityEvent me) {
                    if (back) {
                        for (int i = 0; i < list.length; )
                            // Displays list at origin.
                            System.out.println(i + ": " + list[i++]);
                        // Mission completed.
                        dispose();
                    } else {
                        try {
                            // Obtains directory listing at remote host.
                            list = dir.list();
                            back = true;
                            // Returns to origin.
                            dispatch(origin);
                        } catch (Exception e) {
                            // Failed to return to origin.
                            dispose();
                        }
                    }
                }
            }
        );
        origin = getAgletContext().getHostingURL();
        try {
            dispatch(new URL("atp://killi.genmagic.com"));
        } catch (Exception e) {
            // Failed to dispatch aglet.
        }
    }
}
```

4.9   Summary

We used the aglet's life cycle as the starting point for this chapter and described what can happen to an aglet during its lifetime. The main events in the life of an aglet are creation (*creation* or *cloning*), disposal, mobility (*dispatching* and *retraction*), and persistence (*deactivation* and *activation*).

A delegation-based event model provides uniform handling of these events. When an aglet is cloned, moved, or saved to secondary storage, a number of events are sent to the aglet. An event is propagated from the agent system to an aglet's listener object by invoking a method on the listener and passing the instance of the event subclass that defines the event type generated. The aglet listeners are created by the aglet programmer and provide an elegant way to customize aglet behavior. We also presented several interaction diagrams that illustrate the order of execution and concurrency aspects of the various aglet methods and listener methods.

In Chapter 5, we will describe how an aglet uses the `Aglet Context` interface to manage information within the aglet's context.

Chapter 5
Aglet Context

This chapter covers one of the key elements of the Aglet API: the `AgletContext` interface. You will learn about the methods that an aglet can invoke in its current context in order to create new aglets, retrieve aglets contained in the same context as well as remote contexts, and much more.

An aglet uses the `AgletContext` interface to get information about its environment and to send messages to the environment and to other aglets currently active in that environment. This interface provides a means for maintaining and managing running aglets in an environment where the host system is secured against malicious aglets.

The aglet context is typically created by a server that has a network *daemon* whose job is to monitor the network for aglets. Incoming aglets are received and inserted into the context by the daemon. Often, a user interface component will provide a graphical or command line interface to the context (see Figure 5-1). Tahiti (in Aglets Software Development Kit) is an implementation of this architecture. It provides a graphical user interface that allows you to monitor and control aglets. It contains a network daemon that listens for incoming aglets, and it has a security manager that protects the underlying host. Finally, it instantiates one context.

An aglet belongs at any moment to one and only one context. It can gain access to this context by means of its `getAgletContext` method:

```
context = getAgletContext();
```

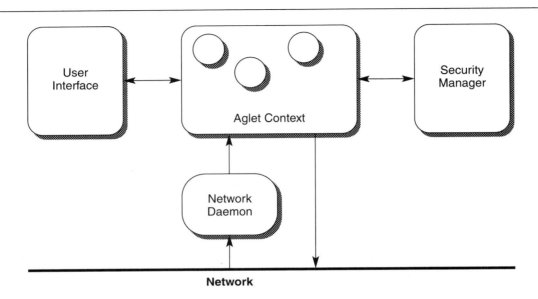

FIGURE 5-1   Aglet Context, User Interface, and Network Daemon

The following sections describe in detail methods for aglet creation, proxy retrieval, and aglet retraction.

5.1   Aglet Creation

The only way you can properly instantiate an aglet is within a context. The context provides all aglets with a uniform initialization and execution environment. That is, an aglet relies on services provided by the context to be properly instantiated and initialized. The createAglet method is used to create new aglets.

```
public abstract AgletProxy AgletContext.createAglet(URL codeBase,
String code, Object init)
```

Creates an instance of the specified aglet class. The aglet's class file can be located on the local file system as well as on a remote server. If codeBase is null, the context will search for the code in the local system's aglet search path (AGLET_PATH).

The createAglet method takes three arguments: codeBase, code, and init.

- codeBase specifies the base URL of the aglet class file—in other words, the (possibly remote) directory that contains the aglet's code. If this argument is null, the directories specified in the local host's aglet search path are searched. The aglet search path works in a similar way to Java's class path.

It is typically an environment variable that specifies a list of directories to be searched for aglet class files.

- code gives the name of the class of the aglet being instantiated.
- init is an object passed on to the aglet's onCreation method.

When an aglet has been successfully created, it is inserted into the current context and started (invocation of onCreation() followed by run()). The method returns a handle (AgletProxy) for the new aglet as soon as the aglet's constructor method finishes.

5.1.1 Code and Code Base

What do we mean by an aglet's code base? It is one of the two arguments necessary to locate the code for an aglet. codeBase specifies by a URL the (possibly remote) directory that contains the aglet's compiled class code. The second argument, code, is always relative to the base URL and translates the Java package dot notation (My.Package.SomeAglet) into a proper path expression (My/Package/SomeAglet.class). Table 5-1 gives examples of code and code base and describes how they are translated into an absolute path for the class file that is being loaded.

What is the purpose of the code base? It plays an important role as a reference point for the aglet's class loader. It is not only used for aglet creation but also used by an aglet when it needs to instantiate new classes (for example, new Some-Class()) during its execution. In this case, the aglet uses the code base to search for the class file of the indicated class. Suppose the code base is http://some.host/path; then the class loader will look for the compiled code of Some-Class on the Web server on some.host with the path path/SomeClass.class (see Figure 5-2).

If the code of SomeClass is located on the local machine, the code base will be something like file://c:/some/path, and the class loader will look for the com-

TABLE 5-1 Code and Code Base

Code Base	Code	Aglet Class File Loaded
file://c:/some/path	Demo	c:\some\path\Demo.class[DOS path]
file://usr/jacob/path	Demo	/usr/jacob/path/Demo.class[UNIX path]
atp://some.host/path	Demo	atp://some.host/path/Demo.class
atp://some.host/test.jar	Demo	Demo.class in the test.jar file
http://www.some.host/path	Demo	http://some.host/path/Demo.class
http://www.some.host/path	Examples.Demo	http://some.host/path/Examples/Demo.class

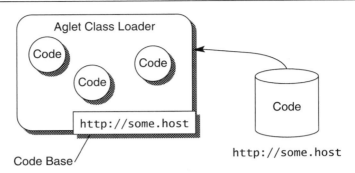

FIGURE 5-2   Code and Code Base

piled code of SomeClass in the file c:\some\path\SomeClass.class. In the special case when the code base is null, the local host's aglet search path (AGLET_PATH) is used. The workings of this search path are very similar to those of Java's class path. It defines a list of directories that are to be searched for the specified class file. Table 5-2 gives two examples in which the code base is null.

Notice that code residing in one of the directories specified in Java's class path cannot move along with an aglet when it is dispatched. In other words, you can regard the code that resides in one of these directories as resident host code. Resident code will typically include the aglet system itself. Obviously, it will also include other installed Java applications, because they are often included in Java's class path when they are installed. The rationale behind this arrangement is to provide an intuitive way of preventing system or application software from moving along with the aglets. Suppose your aglets are using JDBC to access local databases. It really would not be practical to transfer JDBC code from host to host, because that code depends on the type of database located on each host. Instead, the aglet should rely on the local version of JDBC. The environment variables used in the Aglets framework are summarized in Table 5-3.

In the following example we will let the CodeBaseExample aglet create an instance of an aglet whose class code is located in a file named CodeBase-Child.class in the /agletBook/examples directory on a remote Web (http) server named www.some.host:

```
URL codeBase = new URL("http://www.some.host/agletBook/examples");
getAgletContext().createAglet(codeBase, "CodeBaseChild", null);
```

In this case the code base is defined as the URL of the remote host, but what if the code of CodeBaseChild is instead on the local machine? Suppose the code is stored in the local path C:\some\path\CodeBaseChild.class. The solution is simple, because the URL is a powerful abstraction for locations. It covers a wide

TABLE 5-2   Code and Default Code Base

Code Base	Code	Aglet Class File Loaded
null	Demo	[AGLET_PATH]/Demo.class
null	Example.Demo	[AGLET_PATH]/Examples/Demo.class

TABLE 5-3   Aglet Environment Variables

Class Path	Description
CLASSPATH	Classes to be loaded as system classes. These classes will not be transferred with the aglet. In addition, incoming aglets cannot override these classes. For example, Java library classes and Aglets runtime classes (such as AgletProxy and AgletContext) should be placed here.
AGLET_PATH	This is an aglet version of CLASSPATH. AGLET_PATH serves as a default place for aglet classes that are not considered "system" classes (CLASSPATH) and yet are immobile.
AGLET_EXPORT_PATH	This specifies a directory whose subdirectories are accessible from a remote host. The class files and other files that are located in these directories can be fetched from remote aglet servers. Because the fetch mechanism exposes a part of the host's file system, AGLET_EXPORT_PATH has been introduced to control class migration.

range of *schemes*, including file, atp, and http. If the code base is in the local file system, you should use the file URL:

```
file://c:/some/path
```

Table 5-4 summarizes the relationship between the code base URL and the location of the aglet's class file. If the child's class file always shares code base with its creator, you can increase the degree location transparency by replacing the child's absolute code base with the current code base of the creator. This technique is particularly useful when you are developing and testing the aglets in a different environment from the one where they will be deployed. Use the aglet's getCodeBase() to get the current code base:

```
createAglet(getCodeBase(), "ChildAglet", null);
```

5.1.2   Code Base and Class Mobility

Aglets rely on classes from the code base as well as the CLASSPATH. Normally, only the classes from the code base are transferred along with the aglet when it

TABLE 5-4   Code Base URL and File Location

Code Base URL	Location
null	A directory in the aglet search path
file://c:/some/path	A directory (c:/some/path) in the local file system
atp://some.host/some/path	A directory ([AGLET_EXPORT_PATH]/some/path) on a remote aglet server (some.host) using the atp protocol
http://some.host/some/path	A directory on a remote Web server (some.host) using the http protocol

moves in the network. However, not all classes from the code base are transferred at the same time. When an aglet is dispatched to a remote location, only classes in use are transferred. Therefore, when the aglet arrives at the remote location it may require additional classes to continue execution. A network connection is needed for the remote aglet to fetch needed classes from the code base.

A *Java archive* (JAR) file is a file that contains the class and resources, such as image and sound files for a Java program, all gathered into a single file and possibly compressed for faster downloading from a remote host. If a JAR file is specified as code base, however, all classes in the JAR file are transferred at one time along with the aglet. Using a JAR file as code base may lead to transfer of classes that are not used. On the other hand, it does not require fetching of additional classes. If the aglet requires additional classes that are not included in the JAR file, the code base without the JAR file specification is used to fetch the required classes. For example, if the aglet that has the code base `http://some.host/archives/test.jar` needs to instantiate a class not in the JAR file, it can fetch it from `http://some.host/archives`.

5.1.3   Initialization Argument

Notice that the aglet's onCreation method takes a single Object argument. This argument is used to transfer initialization information from the creator to its child. Let us demonstrate this feature by transferring a string of text from the creator (InitExample) and the child (InitChild).

```
public class InitExample extends Aglet {
    public void run() {
        try {
            getAgletContext().createAglet(getCodeBase(),
                                          "InitChild",
                                          "Hello World");
```

```
            } catch (Exception e) {
               System.out.println(e.getMessage());
            }
        }
    }
```

InitExample passes the text string to the child through the third argument in createAglet(). This string is received by InitChild's onCreation method. Because this method is guaranteed to complete its execution before run() is started, it can be trusted to initialize the text field before this field is printed to the console in the run method. Notice that it is necessary to cast the generic init parameter to the actual type of the field (String).

```
public class InitChild extends Aglet {
    String text;  // Uninitialized text field.

    public void onCreation(Object init) {
        // Initialize the text field...
        text = (String)init;
    }

    public void run() {
        // Print the initialized text field...
        System.out.println("The text: \'" + text + "\'");
    }
}
```

5.2   Proxy Retrieval

In this section we will focus on methods that retrieve aglet proxies for you. As you may know, proxies play an important role as convenient handles for aglets. You can use a proxy to gain access to and communicate with its corresponding (possibly remotely located) aglet. We will cover proxies in depth in Chapter 6.

Next, we will demonstrate a number of ways in which you can retrieve proxies from local as well as remotely located aglets.

5.2.1   Proxy Iterator

The first method we will take a closer look at is the getAgletProxies method. This method allows you to iterate the entire set of aglets in the current context.

```
public abstract Enumeration AgletContext.getAgletProxies()
```

Gets the proxies of all aglets in the current context. The resulting list (enumeration) will also include currently deactivated aglets.

In this example we use the getAgletProxies method to list the current set of aglets in the following format:

```
<No.> <Aglet identifier> <Aglet class name>
```

The identity and code name are readily available from the proxy. We can generate this list simply by iterating the set of proxies and for each proxy retrieve the needed information (getAgletID() and getAgletClassName() in the Aglet-Proxy class).

The getAgletProxies method returns an Enumeration of proxies. Enumeration has two methods that support iteration: hasMoreElements() and next-Element(). This excerpt from the ProxyListing example shows how the list is iterated and how aglet information is retrieved and printed on the console:

```
Enumeration e = getAgletContext().getAgletProxies();
int i = 1;  // List counter.
while (e.hasMoreElements()) {
    // Get the proxy.
    AgletProxy proxy = (AgletProxy)e.nextElement();
    // Print a line of aglet information.
    System.out.print("No.: " + i++ + ": ");
    System.out.print(proxy.getAgletID() + " - ");
    System.out.println(proxy.getAgletClassName());
}
```

5.2.2   Getting a Local Proxy

The context also has methods for retrieving the proxy of an aglet if you know the aglet's identity and, if it is not residing in the current context, its location. The first method we will present is used for retrieving the proxy of an aglet in the current context.

> public abstract AgletProxy **AgletContext.getAgletProxy(AgletID identity)**
>
> Gets a proxy for an aglet in the current context. The selected aglet is specified by its identity.

To retrieve a proxy from the current context by the getAgletProxy method, you must know the exact identity of the corresponding aglet. In the following example (see Figure 5-3), we let an aglet create two other aglets. Because one of them is told the identity of the other, it is able to retrieve the proxy of the other and send it a message.

First, the parent aglet (RetrievalExample) creates a child (RetrievalChild1) and stores the child's identifier:

```
AgletProxy proxy = getAgletContext().createAglet(getCodeBase(),
                                                 "RetrievalChild1",
                                                 null);
AgletID aid = proxy.getAgletID();
```

Next, the parent aglet creates a second child (RetrievalChild2), to which it passes the identity (aid) of the first child:

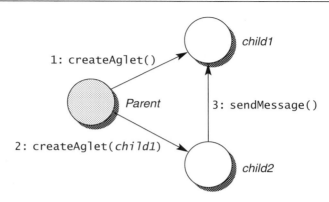

FIGURE 5-3   Local Messaging

```
getAgletContext().createAglet(getCodeBase(),
                              "RetrievalChild2", aid);
```

The behavior of the first child is very simple. With only the handleMessage method implemented, it will respond to any message sent to it by printing the message on the console:

```
public class RetrievalChild1 extends Aglet {
    public boolean handleMessage(Message msg) {
        // Print to the console that you received a message...
        return true;  // Yes, I handled the message.
    }
}
```

The second child's onCreation method takes an aglet identifier as its initialization argument. This identifier is stored in the second child's private aid field and later is used by the run method. In run(), the second child will use the aid field to retrieve the proxy for the first child (also called its *brother*). Having retrieved the proxy, it will send the "Hello brother" message to the first child:

```
public class RetrievalChild2 extends Aglet {
    private AgletID aid;

    public void onCreation(Object init) {
        // Now I know ID of my brother...
        aid = (AgletID)init;
    }

    public void run() {
        // Retrieves the proxy of my brother.
        AgletProxy proxy = getAgletContext().getAgletProxy(aid);
```

```
                        // Sends him a message...
                        proxy.sendMessage(new Message("Hello brother"));
                    }
                }
```

5.2.3   Getting Remote Proxy

Now let us move on to a method that allows us to retrieve the proxy of an aglet hosted in a remote context.

> public abstract AgletProxy **AgletContext.getAgletProxy(URL contextAddress, AgletID identity)**
>
> Gets a proxy for an aglet in a remote context. The remote context is identified by its URL, and the identity indicates the aglet.

To get a proxy of an aglet located in a remote context by using the getAgletProxy method, you must know the URL address of the remote context and the exact identity of the aglet. In the following example, we let an aglet create two aglets (see Figure 5-4). One of these aglets is dispatched to a remote context. Because the other one is told of the location as well as the identity of the remote aglet, it is able to retrieve the proxy of the remote aglet and send it a message.

First, the parent aglet (RemRetrievalExample) creates a child (Retrieval-Child1 is reused from the previous example), stores the child's identifier, and dispatches it to a remote context:

```
AgletProxy proxy = getAgletContext().createAglet(getCodeBase(),
                                                 "RetrievalChild1",
                                                 null);
AgletID aid = proxy.getAgletID();
proxy.dispatch(destination);
```

Next, the parent aglet creates a second child (RemRetrievalChild2), to which it passes the location (destination) and identifier (aid) of the dispatched child:

```
Object args[] = new Object[] { destination, aid };
getAgletContext().createAglet(getCodeBase(),
                              "RemRetrievalChild2", args);
```

The second child's onCreation method takes an aglet's location and identifier as its initialization arguments. This information is stored in the second child's private url and aid fields and is later used by the run method. In run(), the second child will use these fields to retrieve the proxy for the remote aglet. Having retrieved the proxy, it will send the "Hello brother" message to the remote aglet:

```
public class RemRetrievalChild2 extends Aglet {
    private URL url;
    private AgletID aid;
```

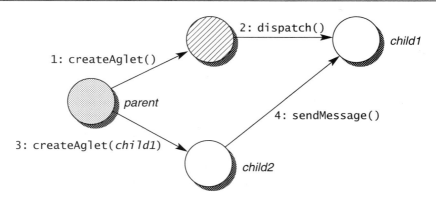

FIGURE 5-4   Remote Messaging

```
public void onCreation(Object init) {
    Object args[] = (Object[])init;
    url = (URL)args[0];
    aid = (AgletID)args[1];
}

public void run() {
    // Retrieves the proxy of my brother.
    AgletProxy proxy = getAgletContext().getAgletProxy(url, aid);
    // Sends him a message...
    try {
        proxy.sendMessage(new Message("Hello brother"));
    }   catch (Exception ex) {
    }
}
```

5.3   Aglet Retraction

In the preceding example we demonstrated how to retrieve the proxy of a remote aglet. If you want the aglet itself, you should use the context's `retractAglet` method. A call to this method in the current context will pull the specified aglet (`identity`) from the specified host (`host`).

> public abstract AgletProxy **AgletContext.retractAglet(URL contextAddress, AgletID identity)**
>
> Retracts an aglet from a remote context to this context and returns its proxy. The remote context is identified by its URL, and the identity indicates the aglet.

We have already briefly introduced you to this method in Chapter 4. `Retraction-Example` demonstrated how to retract an aglet that previously had been dispatched to another aglet server. Here is a code snippet of the example:

```
AgletID aid = proxy.getAgletID();
proxy.dispatch(destination);
getAgletContext().retractAglet(destination, aid);
```

In the first line we store the identity of the aglet (aid); then we dispatch it to the given location (destination), and finally we use retractAglet() to pull it back.

Retraction is a unique feature of the Aglet API, so let us briefly explain the rationale behind it. Consider for moment that you and your aglet server are located behind a corporate *fire wall* (see Figure 5-5). You let your aglets roam the network, which may include servers located *outside* your fire wall. Getting out through the fire wall is generally not a problem. You can, for example, use http tunneling. (By http tunneling we mean a technique by which you can embed another protocol in regular http requests.) The problem is that the fire wall will not allow your aglets to dispatch back to your server waiting *inside* the fire wall. The retraction method allows you to actively pull your aglets back.

There is more to retraction than simply bypassing fire walls. It is also a powerful mechanism for support of *disconnected operation*. Mobile users may dispatch aglets to roam the network during periods when the users themselves are dis-

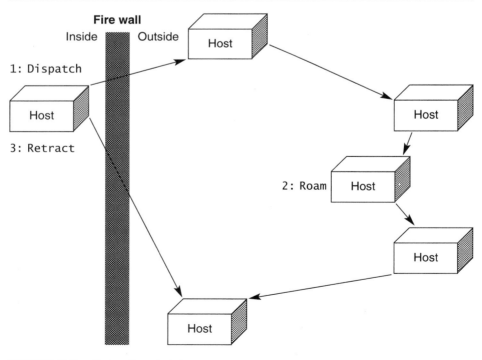

FIGURE 5-5   Retracting Aglets

connected. When and where should an aglet return to when it has finished its task? The `retractAglet` method offers a simple solution to this problem, as we will demonstrate in the following example.

`RetractableAglet` is an aglet that immediately after it has been created dispatches itself to a remote host. Before departing it will leave a fingerprint (its identity) in the current context. At the remote host it will first perform the task it is programmed for. Then the aglet will remain on the remote host and wait for someone (the origin) to retract it.

```java
public class RetractableAglet extends Aglet {
    final int HOME     = 1;
    final int REMOTE    = 2;
    final int BACK_HOME = 3;
    int _status = HOME;

    public void onCreation(Object init) {
        addMobilityListener(
            new MobilityAdapter() {
                public void onDispatching(MobilityEvent e) {
                    // Print to the console...
                }
                public void onArrival(MobilityEvent e) {
                    _status = _status + 1;
                    // Print to the console...
                }
                public void onReverting(MobilityEvent e) {
                    // Print to the console...
                }
            }
        );
    }

    public void run() {
        if (_status == HOME) {
            try {
                getAgletContext().setProperty("agletbook.retractID",
                                            getAgletID());
                dispatch(destination);
            } catch (Exception e) {
                // Failed to dispatch itself.
            }
        } else if (_status == REMOTE) {
            performTask();
        } else if (_status == BACK_HOME) {
            // Print to the console...
        }
    }
}
```

The electronic fingerprint left behind by `RetractableAglet` is its identity stored in the context's properties under the property name `agletbook.retractID`.

At the origin, RetractAglet can be started at any time to retract the remote aglet. Based on the fingerprint that RetractableAglet left behind in the context's property list, RetractAglet will perform a retraction of the aglet waiting at the remote host. After its return to the origin, RetractableAglet reports the result of the task that it performed on the remote host.

```
public class RetractAglet extends Aglet {
    public void run() {
        try {
            AgletID aid = AgletID)getAgletContext().getProperty(
                              "agletbook.retractID");
            getAgletContext().retractAglet(destination, aid);
        } catch (Exception e) {
            // Failed to retract the aglet.
        }
    }
}
```

5.4   Context Properties

The final feature of the context that we would like to introduce is the property that allows aglets to leave electronic fingerprints when they roam the network. The property list is a list of attribute-value pairs.

Three methods are available for managing properties. You retrieve the value of a property by using the getProperty method, and you add and update properties by using the setProperty method.

public abstract Object **AgletContext.getProperty(String key)**

Gets the context property indicated by the key.

public abstract Object **AgletContext.getProperty(String key, Object def)**

Gets the context property indicated by the key and default value.

public abstract void **AgletContext.setProperty(String key, Object value)**

Sets the context property indicated by the key and value.

It is straightforward to set a property or leave a fingerprint. This code snippet is taken from RetractableAglet, which leaves its identity behind before it leaves the context:

```
getAgletContext().setProperty("agletbook.retractID",
                              getAgletID());
```

Later, another aglet can retrieve the aglet identifier from this property:

```
aid = (AgletID)getAgletContext().getProperty("agletbook.retractID");
```

5.5 Aglet Example: Directory Listing

Let us conclude this chapter with a practical aglet that can be sent out to capture a directory listing on a remote host and then retracted by the origin to display the listing (see Figure 5-6).

ListingAglet has three instance variables: retracted, which is a Boolean variable that is false before retraction and true after the aglet has been retracted; dir, which contains path information for the directory listing; and list, which contains the result of the directory listing.

The aglet implements the onCreation method, which initializes the dir variable from its init argument as given by the creator of the aglet. It also installs a mobility listener that handles two events: onArrival() and onReverting(). When the aglet arrives at the remote host, retracted is false, and, assuming that the aglet is given the proper security permissions, it will capture the local directory listing in list. When the aglet is retracted, retracted is set to true. When the aglet arrives at the origin, it will display the directory listing.

```
public class ListingAglet extends Aglet {
    boolean retracted = false;
    File dir = null;
    String[] list;
```

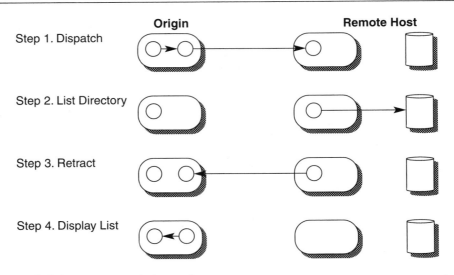

FIGURE 5-6   Directory Listing Aglet

```
public void onCreation(Object init) {
    dir = (File)init;
    addMobilityListener(
        new MobilityAdapter() {
            public void onArrival(MobilityEvent me) {
                try {
                    if (retracted) {
                        // Displays list at origin.
                        for (int i = 0; i < list.length; )
                        System.out.println(i + ": " + list[i++]);
                    } else {
                        // Obtains directory listing at remote host.
                        list = dir.list();
                    }
                } catch (Exception e) {
                    dispose();
                }
            }
            public void onReverting(MobilityEvent me) {
                retracted = true;
            }
        }
    );
}
```

In the following code we show you how to create and set up the Listing-
Aglet. The creator can be, for example, a stationary aglet. In the first two lines,
the destination and directory path are set. Then ListingAglet is created with the
directory path as the initialization argument. When the aglet has been created, it
is first dispatched to the destination host and then immediately retracted. When
the aglet returns, it is disposed of.

```
URL destination = new URL(destination);
File directory = new File("C:\PUBLIC");
AgletProxy proxy = getAgletContext().createAglet(getCodeBase(),
                                                 "ListingAglet",
                                                 directory);
proxy = proxy.dispatch(destination);
proxy = getAgletContext().retractAglet(destination,proxy.
                                       getAgletID());
proxy.dispose();
```

The use of retraction in this example allows the aglet to travel from inside a fire
wall to the outside to obtain information. The retracted aglet will then bring the
obtained information with it inside the fire wall.

5.6 Summary

We have introduced you to the `AgletContext` interface, which is used by an aglet to get information about its environment and to send messages to the environment and other aglets currently active in that environment.

We have covered the facets of aglet creation and related concepts such as code location, code base, class mobility, and aglet initialization. To provide access to aglets in a context, you can retrieve handles (proxies) that allow you to send messages to the aglets. We have shown how to use a proxy iterator to traverse all aglets in a context. We have also shown how to retrieve a proxy of a specific local as well as remote aglet.

Retraction is a unique feature of the Aglet API. It lets your aglets roam the network while you can at any time actively pull your aglets back to your server. It is a powerful mechanism for support of disconnected operation. Mobile users can dispatch aglets to roam the network during periods when the users themselves are disconnected.

In Chapter 6, we turn to the topic of aglet messaging, the means by which aglets communicate.

Chapter 6
Aglet Messaging

An important property of aglets is that they can communicate with one another. Interaglet communication is supported by a rich framework in which aglets that do not necessarily "know" each other can exchange messages. An aglet may often need to cooperate with aglets developed by other organizations. It isn't likely that the cooperating aglets in such a collection were developed at the same time or are even known to each other at compile time. As a result, we need an interaction and communication model that is richer, more flexible, and more extensible than that used in normal method invocation.

The aglet supports an object-based messaging framework that is (1) location-independent, (2) extensible, (3) rich, and (4) synchronous/asynchronous. In this chapter you will learn about the basics of aglet messaging. Several means of interaglet communication are supported, and you will learn about simple messaging with and without reply, advanced message management, and multicast messaging between aglets.

6.1 Simple Messaging

The principal way for aglets to communicate is by message passing. Interaglet messaging is based on a simple event scheme that requires an aglet to implement handlers only for the kinds of messages that it is supposed to understand. The message-handling method in the Aglet class is called handleMessage. You do not call this method directly when you wish to send a message to an aglet. Instead, you invoke the sendMessage method on the proxy, which serves as a message gateway for the aglet (see Figure 6-1). One of the benefits of using the proxy is that it provides you with a location-independent interface for sending messages to aglets. In other words, it does not matter whether you are using a remote proxy (a proxy for a remote aglet) or a local proxy to send a message; the interface (sendMessage()) is the same.

The sendMessage method of the proxy takes a message object as an argument and sends the message to the aglet for which the proxy is acting as a gateway. The method may return an object in reply to the message.

public Object **AgletProxy.sendMessage(Message message)**

Sends a message object to the aglet and waits for the aglet to reply.

In the following code, SimpleMessageExample creates a simple message object of the "Hello" kind and sends it to an aglet, SimpleMessageChild. In this example we are not interested in the reply to the message and will therefore simply ignore the result returned by sendMessage():

```
public class SimpleMessageExample extends Aglet {
    public void run() {
        try {
            AgletProxy proxy = getAgletContext().createAglet(
                            getCodeBase(),
                            "SimpleMessageChild",
                            null);
            try {
                proxy.sendMessage(new Message("Hello"));
            } catch (NotHandledException e) {
                // Child failed to handle the message.
            }
```

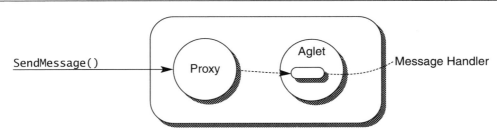

FIGURE 6-1 Simple Messaging

```
        } catch (Exception e) {
            // Failed to create the child.
        }
    }
}
```

The `handleMessage` method of the `Aglet` class is one of the key methods that the aglet programmer is supposed to override. It enables the aglet to respond to messages sent to it. Typically, the implementation of this method will consist of a switch statement that tests for the kind of the incoming message. Notice that the handler is supposed to return a Boolean value: `true` if the message kind was understood and handled, or `false` if the message kind was neither understood nor handled.

```
public boolean Aglet.handleMessage(Message message)
```
Handles an incoming message object.

This simple message handler in `SimpleMessageChild` accepts and handles messages of the `"Hello"` kind. To acknowledge that it has handled such a message, it returns the Boolean value `true`. It will reject all other kinds of messages by returning the value `false`.

```
public class SimpleMessageChild extends Aglet {

    public boolean handleMessage(Message msg) {
        if (msg.sameKind("Hello")) {
            doHello();          // Respond to the 'hello' message...
            return true;        // Yes, I handled this message.
        } else
            return false;       // No, I did not handle this message.
    }
}
```

Now what will happen if we send a message to an aglet that it is not prepared to handle? Let us take the `SimpleMessageExample` and introduce a typo in the message's `kind` field.

```
proxy.sendMessage(new Message("Helo"));
```

In this case, `handleMessage()` in `SimpleMessageChild` will not recognize the message kind and will instantly return the value `false`. Back in the `Simple-MessageExample` aglet we will now experience a `NotHandledException`. The moral for message senders: always be prepared to catch a `NotHandledException`.

6.2 The Message Class

Messages are objects (see Figure 6-2). A message object is characterized by its *kind*. This string property is used to distinguish messages from each other. The `Message` class supports a range of constructors that all have `kind` as a mandatory

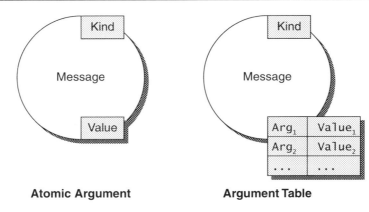

Atomic Argument   **Argument Table**

FIGURE 6-2   Message Objects

argument. Message objects also contain an optional argument field for data associated with a particular message. The argument field can be either atomic (String, int, etc.) or tabular (Hashtable).

6.2.1   Message Creation

The many message constructors represent shortcuts for the initialization of the argument field.

public **Message(String kind)**

Constructs a message of the specified kind. Creates by default an argument table that can hold a set of key-value pairs. The setArg method can be used to initialize the argument hash table.

public **Message(String kind, Object arg)**

Constructs a message of the specified kind with an initial binding of the Object argument.

public **Message(String kind, int arg)**

Constructs a message of the specified kind and with an initial binding of the int argument.

public **Message(String kind, long arg)**

Constructs a message of the specified kind and with an initial binding of the long argument.

public **Message(String kind, float arg)**

Constructs a message of the specified kind and with an initial binding of the float argument.

public **Message(String kind, double arg)**

Constructs a message of the specified kind and with an initial binding of the double argument.

Public **Message(String kind, char arg)**

Constructs a message of the specified kind and with an initial binding of the char argument.

public **Message(String kind, boolean arg)**

Constructs a message of the specified kind and with an initial binding of the boolean argument.

We will now look at a few examples of typical message objects. The first one shows the construction of a simple message of the "Hello" kind:

```
Message msg = new Message("Hello");
```

The second example shows the creation of a "Greeting" message with the string "Happy Birthday" as argument:

```
Message msg = new Message("Greeting", "Happy Birthday");
```

The final example of a simple message object is as follows:

```
Message msg = new Message("Height", 175);
```

The constructors initialize two fields in the message object. The first field is kind, a String field that indicates the kind of the message. The second field is arg, an Object field that holds the argument object of the message.

As an example, let us take the MessageExample aglet that creates and sends three different kinds of messages to the MessageChild aglet: "Hello", "Greeting", and "Height".

```
public class MessageExample extends Aglet {
    public void run() {
        try {
            AgletProxy proxy = getAgletContext().createAglet(
                                    getCodeBase(),
                                    "MessageChild", null);
            try {
                proxy.sendMessage(new Message("Hello"));
                proxy.sendMessage(new Message(
                                    "Greeting","Happy Birthday"));
                proxy.sendMessage(new Message("Height", 175));
            } catch (Exception e) {
                // Child failed to handle message.
            }
        } catch (Exception e) {
            // Failed to create the child.
        }
    }
}
```

6.2.2   Receiving Messages

Messages are received by an aglet's message handler (handleMessage()). The first task of the message handler is to determine the kind of the message either by retrieving the kind field (getKind()) or by using the sameKind method. Having determined the kind of the message, the handler can now retrieve a possible argument from the message by using the getArg method.

public String **Message.getKind()**

Gets the kind of the message.

public boolean **Message.sameKind(String)**

Compares the kind of the message with the string argument.

public Object **Message.getArg()**

Gets the argument object of the message.

MessageChild shows how to implement a trivial handler for the different kinds of messages. The sameKind method is used to distinguish the different messages. This example also demonstrates how to retrieve the message argument (getArg()) from the message object.

```
public class MessageChild extends Aglet {
    public boolean handleMessage(Message msg) {
        if (msg.sameKind("Hello"))
           print("Handling \'Hello\': ");
        else if (msg.sameKind("Greeting"))
           print("handling \'Greeting\': " + msg.getArg());
        else if (msg.sameKind("Height")) {
           int height = ((Integer)msg.getArg()).intValue();
           print("handling \'Height\': " + height);
        } else {
           return false;
        }
        return true;  // Yes, I did handle the message.
    }
}
```

The Message class has two methods for handling messages with nonatomic arguments. The reason is that messages often need to carry multiple arguments to the receivers. Such arguments are most effectively handled as key-value pairs. The setArg and getArg methods are convenient for organizing multiple arguments into a table.

public void **Message.setArg(String key, Object value)**

Maps the specified key to the specified value in the argument table.

Public Object **Message.getArg(String key)**

Gets the value to which the key is mapped in the argument table; this value is null if the key is not mapped to any value in the argument table.

Suppose you want to send a "Location" message to an aglet. This message requires two arguments (Horizontal and Vertical) to advertise the location. We use setArg() to create two key-value pairs in the message object.

```
public class MessageHashExample extends Aglet {
    public void run() {
        try {
            AgletProxy proxy = getAgletContext().createAglet(
                                getCodeBase(),
                                "MessageHashChild", null);
            try {
                Message msg = new Message("Location");
                msg.setArg("Horizontal", 40);
                msg.setArg("Vertical", 60);
                proxy.sendMessage(msg);
            } catch (Exception e) {
                // Failed to send the message.
            }
        } catch (Exception e) {
            // Failed to create the child.
        }
    }
}
```

The message handler in MessageHashChild can now retrieve the advertised location by means of the two keys: Horizontal and Vertical.

```
public class MessageHashChild extends Aglet {
    public boolean handleMessage(Message msg) {
        if (msg.sameKind("Location")) {
            int h = ((Integer)msg.getArg("Horizontal")).intValue();
            int v = ((Integer)msg.getArg("Vertical")).intValue();
            print("Handling \'Location\': (" + h + "," + v + ")");
            return true;
        }
        return false;
    }
}
```

6.2.3 Replying to Messages

The final group of methods in the Message class that will be described in this section is aimed at message handlers that want to reply to incoming messages. The message handler uses the incoming message object to deliver a reply to the message. The sendReply method of the message object is used to acknowledge the message (see Figure 6-3).

There are several sendReply methods. The first of them does not take any arguments. It is used to send a reply without any specific value. The receiver of an "empty" reply receives the value null. All the others take one argument: the reply.

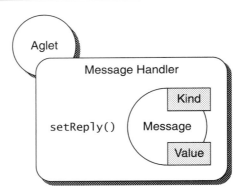

FIGURE 6-3   Message Reply

```
public void Message.sendReply()
```
Sends a reply without any specific value. The message sender will receive a
null value from this reply.

```
Public void Message.sendReply(Object reply)
```
Sends an object reply.

```
Public void Message.sendReply(int reply)
```
Sends a numeric reply.

```
Public void Message.sendReply(long reply)
```
Sends a numeric reply.

```
Public void Message.sendReply(float reply)
```
Sends a numeric reply.

```
Public void Message.sendReply(double reply)
```
Sends a numeric reply.

```
Public void Message.sendReply(char reply)
```
Sends a character reply.

```
public void Message.sendReply(boolean reply)
```
Sends a Boolean reply.

It is time for an example that demonstrates how a message handler responds
to an incoming message. When the following message handler receives the "What
is your height?" message, it is supposed to respond to that message with an
integer reply. If its "height" is, say, 175, it can create a reply with the numeric

value 175. The way that the (possibly remote) sender of the message will receive and process that reply will be covered in a few moments (we will return to the `ReplyExample` aglet later in this chapter).

```java
public class ReplyChild extends Aglet {
    public boolean handleMessage(Message msg) {
        if (msg.sameKind("What is your height?")) {
            msg.sendReply(175);  // Replies to the message.
        }
        return true;  // Yes, I handled this message.
    }
}
```

But what if the message handler fails while handling a message? So far we have treated message handling in a black-and-white manner: a message is either handled or it is not handled. Obviously, message handling can also lead to exceptions being thrown. In that case, the message handler should not merely return the Boolean value `false` to indicate that the message was not handled; instead, it should reply with an exception stating the cause of the failure. For this purpose the `sendReply` method is paired with the `sendException` method.

public void **Message.sendException(Exception exception)**

Replies with an exception.

Let the `ExceptionExample` aglet send a "`Set the height`" message to its child aglet. This kind of message carries an integer argument. The sender aglet is ready to catch the `MessageException` in case the child decides to reply to this message with an exception.

```java
public class ExceptionExample extends Aglet {
    public void run() {
        try {
            AgletProxy proxy = getAgletContext().createAglet(
                                    getCodeBase(),
                                    "ExceptionChild",
                                    null);
            try {
                proxy.sendMessage(new Message("Set the height", -100));
            } catch (MessageException e) {
                // Message handling resulted in an exception.
            }
        } catch (Exception e) {
            // Failed to create the child.
        }
    }
}
```

The message handler in `ExceptionChild` accepts "`Set the height`" messages carrying an integer argument. It is reasonable, however, for the message handler to reject negative integer values. If a negative height is given, the handler will respond to the message with an exception:

```
public class ExceptionChild extends Aglet {
   public boolean handleMessage(Message msg) {
      if (msg.sameKind("Set the height")) {
         if (((Integer)msg.getArg().intValue() < 0) {
            // Hmm, invalid value for 'height'.
            msg.sendException(new Exception("Illegal value"));
         }
         doSomething();
         return true;   // Yes, I did handle this message.
      }
      return false;     // No, I did not handle this message.
   }
}
```

6.3 Getting the Reply

We will now continue to describe how the sender of a message receives and processes a reply. There are basically two ways this is done: *synchronously* and *asynchronously*. In synchronous messaging (see Figure 6-4), the sender of the message suspends its execution until a reply has arrived. In asynchronous messaging (see Figure 6-5), the sender continues its execution and subsequently retrieves the reply. We also call this *nonblocking* messaging.

6.3.1 Synchronous Messaging

The proxy's sendMessage method (introduced earlier in this chapter) is used for synchronous messaging. An invocation of this method will block further execution until a reply or an exception has been received.

In the following example, the ReplyExample aglet sends the message "What is your height?" to the proxy of the ReplyChild aglet. The execution of the

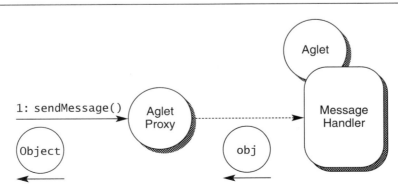

FIGURE 6-4   Synchronous Messaging

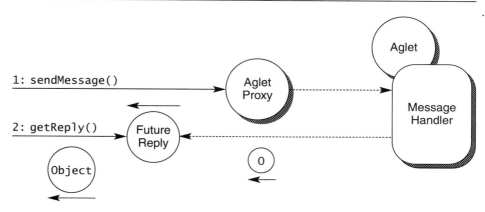

FIGURE 6-5   Asynchronous Messaging

message sender halts until it receives a reply. Because the return type of send-Message() is Object, it is necessary to cast the reply to the expected reply type. In this example the reply type is an Integer object.

```
public class ReplyExample extends Aglet {
    public void run() {
        try {
            AgletProxy proxy = getAgletContext().createAglet(
                                getCodeBase(),
                                "ReplyChild",
                                null);
            try {
                Object reply = proxy.sendMessage(
                                new Message("What is your height?"));
                int height = ((Integer)reply).intValue();
                print("Her height is: " + height);
            } catch (Exception e) {
                // Failed to send the message.
            }
        } catch (Exception e) {
            // Failed to create the child.
        }
    }
}
```

6.3.2   Asynchronous Messaging

Asynchronous messaging in the Aglet API is based on the idea a *future* object. The future object, which is returned by the proxy's sendFutureMessage method, serves as a handle for the expected reply to the message. The object is called a *future* because it is returned immediately to the sender of the message, bearing the promise of a future reply.

> public FutureReply **AgletProxy.sendFutureMessage(Message message)**
>
> Sends a message object to the aglet and gets a future reply object.

The group of methods in the FutureReply class that we cover in this section is related to nonblocking retrieval of the reply to a message. Nonblocking, or asynchronous, messaging allows you to continue execution while the reply has not yet arrived. The first method, isAvailable(), allows you to test whether the reply has come. It returns true if the reply is ready and can be retrieved without blocking continued execution. The waitForReply methods allow the current thread to wait a specified period of time for a reply. Finally, the getReply method gets the reply when it is available.

> public boolean **FutureReply.isAvailable()**
>
> Checks whether a reply has arrived.

> public void **FutureReply.waitForReply(long duration)**
>
> Waits for a reply to arrive. If the reply arrives within the specified period of time, the thread will continue its execution. Otherwise, the execution will continue when the specified period of time has elapsed.

> Public void **FutureReply.waitForReply()**
>
> Waits for a reply to arrive before it continues execution.

> public Object **FutureReply.getReply()**
>
> Gets the reply to the message. This method will block until a reply can be returned.

The following example demonstrates how the aglet can proceed with a given task from the moment a message is sent until a reply has arrived. In this example, we have created a small loop that uses the isAvailable method to test whether a reply has arrived. As long as no reply has arrived, the body of the loop (doIncrement()) will be executed repeatedly:

```
public class FutureExample extends Aglet {
    public void run() {
        try {
            AgletProxy proxy = getAgletContext().createAglet(
                            getCodeBase(), "FutureChild",
                            null);
            try {
                FutureReply future = proxy.sendFutureMessage(
                            new Message("Please reply"));
                while (!future.isAvailable())
                    doIncrement();
```

```
                    String reply = (String)future.getReply();
                } catch (NotHandledException e) {
                    // Failed to send the message.
                }
            } catch (Exception e) {
                // Failed to create the child.
            }
        }
    }
```

In another typical case of asynchronous messaging, we wish to avoid being trapped in a call to getReply that may never return. This can happen when the message handler goes into a nonterminating loop or when a deadlock occurs. The following example shows how to wait a limited period of time for a reply. The example uses the waitForReply method, which takes a time-out argument. The waitForReply method will block until either a reply has arrived or the timer expires. Because we cannot tell why waitForReply() returns, an additional call to isAvailable() is needed:

```
public class TimeoutExample extends Aglet {
    public void run() {
        try {
            AgletProxy proxy = getAgletContext().createAglet(
                            getCodeBase(),
                            "TimeoutChild",
                            null);
            try {
                FutureReply future = proxy.sendFutureMessage(
                            new Message("Please reply"));
                future.waitForReply(4000);  // Wait up to 4 seconds.
                if (future.isAvailable()) {
                    String reply = (String)future.getReply();
                    // Got the reply...
                } else
                    // Time out... Forget the reply.
            } catch (NotHandledException e) {
                // Failed to send the message.
            }

        } catch (Exception e) {
            // Failed to create the child.
        }
    }
}
```

6.4 Message Management

Each aglet has a guard, called the message manager, that allows deterministic message handling by inserting incoming messages into a queue (see Figure 6-6). It forwards these messages one at a time to the aglet's message handler in the

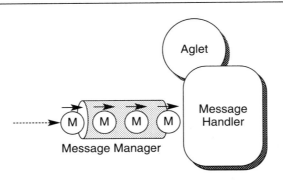

FIGURE 6-6 Message Manager

same order that they were received. It also ensures that the next message is not forwarded until the current message has been handled. Technically, the message manager *serializes* message handling.

The message manager features a number of methods that enable the aglet to customize the behavior of the message manager. This set of methods includes the ability of the aglet to serialize messages, to prioritize messages by their kind, to allow parallel message handling, and to synchronize incoming messages.

6.4.1 Serialized Message Handling

Let us start our coverage of the message manager by taking a look at message serialization. The following example demonstrates serialized message handling. One aglet (`MsgManagerExample`) sends three consecutive messages (`"One"`, `"Two"`, and `"Three"`) to another aglet (`MsgManagerChild`):

```
public class MsgManagerExample extends Aglet {
    public void run() {
        try {
            AgletProxy proxy = getAgletContext().createAglet(
                            getCodeBase(),
                            "MsgManagerChild",
                            null);
            try {
                proxy.sendFutureMessage(new Message("One"));
                proxy.sendFutureMessage(new Message("Two"));
                proxy.sendFutureMessage(new Message("Three"));
            } catch (Exception e) {
                // Failed to send a message.
            }
```

```
            } catch (Exception e) {
                // Failed to create the child.
            }
        }
    }
```

Messages are handled deterministically; that is, the `MsgManagerChild` aglet will not start handling one message before it has completed the handling of the previous message. In this example, the aglet will not start handling message "Two" until it has finished handling message "One", and it will not start handling message "Three" until it has finished handling message "Two":

```
public class MsgManagerChild extends Aglet {
    public boolean handleMessage(Message msg) {
        if (msg.sameKind("One")) {
            // Does something...
            return true;
        } else if (msg.sameKind("Two")) {
            // Does something...
            return true;
        } else if (msg.sameKind("Three")) {
            // Does something...
            return true;
        }
        return false;
    }
}
```

The interaction chart in Figure 6-7 illustrates the execution trace of this example.

6.4.2 Message Priorities

The rest of this section covers the advanced use of the message manager. As a first step, the aglet must access its message manager. This is done through the `get-MessageManager` method defined in the aglet's own interface.

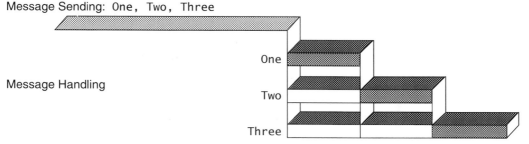

FIGURE 6-7   Interaction Chart for Serialized Message Handling

```
public final MessageManager Aglet.getMessageManager()
```
Gets the message manager.

Now that we have access to the message manager, we will demonstrate how it allows you to set the priority of specific kinds of messages. Setting a high priority for a given kind of message will ensure that it is placed in the message queue ahead of messages with a lower priority. The default priority of a message is 5. The priority range is 1 to 10. You use the setPriority method in Message-Manager class to set a user-defined priority.

```
public void MessageManager.setPriority(String kind, int
priority)
```
Sets the message's priority. The default priority for messages is 5.

To demonstrate the effect of this method, we will create a variant of the preceding message-handling aglet; this one raises the priority of message "Three". The objective is to increase the likelihood that message "Three" is handled before message "Two". The default priority of a message is 5, so let us raise the priority of message "Three" to 10. We conveniently raise the priority in the message-handling aglet's (MsgPriorityChild) onCreation method:

```
public class MsgPriorityChild extends Aglet {
    public void onCreation(Object obj) {
        getMessageManager().setPriority("Three", 10);
    }

    public boolean handleMessage(Message msg) {
        // Handles incoming messages...
    }
}
```

The interaction chart in Figure 6-8 illustrates the most likely execution trace of this example. (The order in which messages are received is not deterministic because of the concurrent nature of the system.)

6.4.3   Parallel Message Handling

The message manager also allows messages to be handled in parallel. Calling the exitMonitor method enables the aglet to continue the current message-handling thread while simultaneously allowing a new message-handling thread to be started. Note that only the thread that owns the monitor can call this method. For all of the other threads, this results in an exception (IllegalMonitorState-Exception).

```
public void MessageManager.exitMonitor()
```
Exits the current monitor.

Message Sending: One, Two, Three

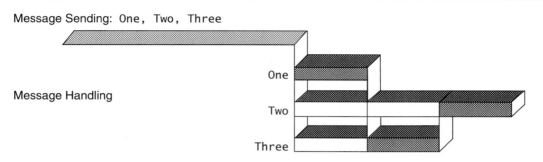

Message Handling

FIGURE 6-8 Interaction Chart for Prioritized Message Handling

In the MsgParallelChild aglet's handling of the message "Two", we explicitly allow other messages to be handled in parallel. When the aglet starts handling the message "Two", it immediately exits the monitor (exitMonitor()). While it continues to handle the message "Two", it will concurrently start handling the next message in the queue, "Three".

```
public class MsgParallelChild extends Aglet {
    public boolean handleMessage(Message msg) {
        if (msg.sameKind("One")) {
            // Does something...
            return true;
        } else if (msg.sameKind("Two")) {
            // Starting...
            getMessageManager().exitMonitor();
            // Continuing...
            return true;
        } else if (msg.sameKind("Three")) {
            // Does something...
            return true;
        }
        return false;
    }
}
```

Figure 6-9 shows the aglet simultaneously handling messages "Two" and "Three".

6.4.4 Synchronized Message Handling

If the handling of a message cannot proceed for some reason (possibly external), the current thread can be suspended until further notice. In this way, it will not

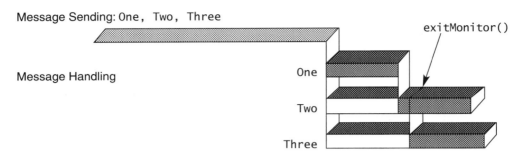

FIGURE 6-9   Interaction Chart for Parallel Message Handling

block the handling of subsequent messages. For this purpose, the aglet defines three methods: waitMessage(), notifyMessage(), and notifyAllMessages().

public void **Aglet.waitMessage()**

Suspends the execution of this message-handling thread. The thread waits until further notice.

Public void **Aglet.notifyMessage()**

Notifies a single waiting message thread in this aglet's message manager.

Public void **Aglet.notifyAllMessages()**

Notifies all waiting message threads in this aglet's message manager.

This example aglet, MsgWaitingChild, suspends the execution of the message-handling thread of message "Two". This allows the aglet to handle message "Three", which subsequently will instruct the message manager to resume execution of the waiting message-handling thread.

```
public class MsgWaitingChild extends Aglet {
    public boolean handleMessage(Message msg) {
        if (msg.sameKind("One")) {
            // Does something...
            return true;
        } else if (msg.sameKind("Two")) {
            // Starting...
            waitMessage();
            // Continuing...
            return true;
        } else if (msg.sameKind("Three")) {
            // Starting...
            pause();
            notifyMessage();
```

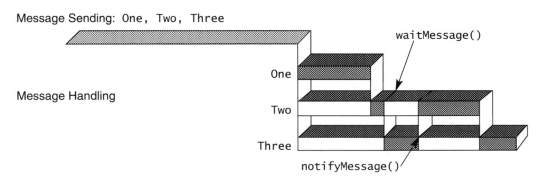

Message Sending: One, Two, Three

Message Handling

waitMessage()

One

Two

Three

notifyMessage()

FIGURE 6-10   Interaction Chart for Synchronized Message Handling

```
            // Continuing...
            return true;
        }
        return false;
    }
}
```

The interaction chart for this example is shown in Figure 6-10.

6.5   **Remote Messaging**

Aglets support remote message passing, and they can communicate through messages remotely as well as locally. Any arguments and return values passed by remote messaging can be of any Java type that is serializable. Sending a remote message is different from dispatching an aglet in the sense that a remote message does not cause any transfer of byte code, and therefore the classes used in the message must be installed in both hosts.

Although remote message passing can be used as a lightweight way of communicating between aglets that reside on different hosts, dispatching an aglet can take advantage of locality—for example, disconnected operations or intensive interaction with hosts.

Remote message passing is easy with the Aglet API, because the methods that you use for remote message passing are exactly the same as those for local messaging. Therefore, we can say that messaging between aglets is location-transparent.

6.6   Multicasting

So far we have dealt only with peer-to-peer messaging, in which the message sender must know either the proxy or the identity of the receiver. You will often find this requirement a limitation when you plan to coordinate activities among multiple aglets. In such cases, each aglet may not be aware of the identities of the other aglets. Just imagine multiple aglets originating from different sources that meet in a specific context. How does an incoming aglet advertise its arrival? Fortunately, the context supports message *multicasting* within a single context (see Figure 6-11). Message multicasting provides a powerful way for aglets to interact and collaborate. The basic principle is that aglets (1) subscribe to one or more multicast messages and (2) implement handlers for these messages.

Aglets subscribe to specific multicast messages by invoking the `subscribe-Message` method with the message kind as argument. Aglets can subscribe to multiple multicast messages. To unsubscribe, the aglet must invoke `unsubscribeMessage()` for the specific message kind. It can also unsubscribe to all multicast messages by invoking `unsubscribeAllMessages()`. When an aglet leaves its current context it will automatically unsubscribe to all messages.

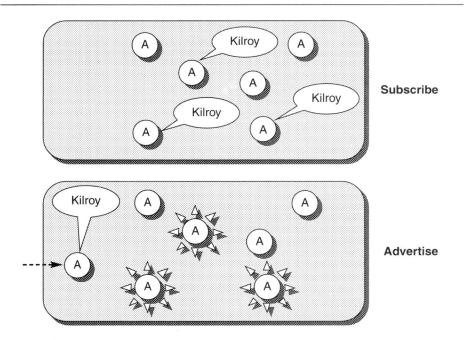

FIGURE 6-11   Multicasting

```
public final void Aglet.subscribeMessage(String kind)
```

Subscribes to one kind of multicast message.

```
public final boolean Aglet.unsubscribeMessage(String
kind)
```

Unsubscribes to one kind of multicast message.

```
public final void Aglet.unsubscribeAllMessages()
```

Unsubscribes to all kinds of multicast messages.

In the following example, the MulticastSubscriber aglet automatically subscribes to "Hello Everybody" when it is created (onCreation()). It also implements a handler for the "Hello Everybody" multicast message (handleMessage()).

```
public class MulticastSubscriber extends Aglet {
    public void onCreation(Object o) {
        subscribeMessage("Hello Everybody");
    }

    public boolean handleMessage(Message msg) {
        if (msg.sameKind("Hello Everybody")) {
            // Does something...
            return true;
        }
        return false;
    }
}
```

Now let us switch to the context class that defines the multicastMessage method in the AgletContext class. This method takes a message object as argument and sends it to subscribers to the multicast message in the current context. The message object for multicast messaging is identical to the one used for normal messaging. A notable difference between multicast messaging and normal aglet messaging is that multicast messaging is local to a context. In other words, multicast messaging is not location-transparent.

```
public ReplySet AgletContext.multicastMessage(Message
message)
```

Sends a multicast message to the subscribers in the current context.

The following code example (MulticastExample) shows how an aglet sends "Hello Everybody" as a multicast message in its current context. It does not expect any replies from the subscribers.

```
public class MulticastExample extends Aglet {
    public void run() {
        try {
```

```
                getAgletContext().createAglet(getCodeBase(),
                                              "MulticastSubscriber",
                                              null);
                ... // Creates multiple instances of 'MulticastSubscriber'.
                Message msg = new Message("Hello Everybody");
                getAgletContext().multicastMessage(msg);
            } catch (Exception e) {
                // Failed to create a subscriber.
            }
        }
    }
```

6.7   Receiving Multiple Replies

Let us conclude this chapter by introducing the ReplySet class. This class can be used to hold multiple FutureReply objects. It is a simple, powerful concept that allows you to manage replies from multiple aglets. The context's multicast-Message method returns a reply set that allows the sender to retrieve possible replies from the subscribers.

The ReplySet class features two methods that allow you to retrieve replies from the reply set. The hasMoreReplies method checks whether there are any FutureReply objects left in the reply set. The getNextFutureReply method gets the next FutureReply object whose reply is available.

public boolean **ReplySet.hasMoreReplies()**

Checks whether there are more FutureReply objects in the set.

public FutureReply **ReplySet.getNextFutureReply()**

Gets the next FutureReply object whose reply is available.

The following example shows how to use the ReplySet class in connection with multicast messaging. The ReplySetExample aglet creates multiple instances of the ReplySetChild aglet. It then sends a multicast message to all its children and gets a reply set in return. The hasMoreFutureReplies and the getNextReply methods are used to iterate the reply set and retrieve each reply.

```
public class ReplySetExample extends Aglet {
    public void run() {
        try {
            getAgletContext().createAglet(
                                getCodeBase(), "ReplySetChild",
                                null);
            ... // Creates multiple instances of 'ReplySetChild'.
            try {
```

```
                          Message msg = new Message("Hello Everybody");
                          ReplySet replies= getAgletContext().multicast
                                            Message(msg);
                          while (replies.hasMoreFutureReplies()) {
                              FutureReply future = replies.getNextFutureReply();
                              print((String)future.getReply());
                          }
                    } catch (Exception e) {
                        // Failed to multicast the message.
                    }
                } catch (Exception e) {
                    // Failed to create a subscriber.
                }
            }
        }
```

Each child simply replies to the message by a sendReply():

```
    public class ReplySetChild extends Aglet {
        public void onCreation(Object o) {
            ... // Subscribes to the 'Hello Everybody' message.
        }

        public boolean handleMessage(Message msg) {
            if (msg.sameKind("Hello Everybody")) {
                msg.sendReply(someReply);
                return true;
            }
            return false;
        }
    }
```

There is even a way to manually add additional FutureReply objects to the reply set. This approach broadens the use of reply sets to include regular future-based messaging.

```
    public boolean ReplySet.addFutureReply(FutureReply)
```

Adds the FutureReply object to the reply set.

6.8   Aglet Example: Directory Listing

Let us for a moment return to the directory listing aglet example in Chapter 5. That example showed a practical aglet that could be sent out to capture a directory listing on a remote host and then retracted by the origin to display the listing. Now let us look at a different approach to solve the same task (remote directory listing), this time using messaging as an alternative to retraction.

In Figure 6-12 we show that the aglet is first sent to the remote host. Then it captures the directory information and sends a message to the origin containing

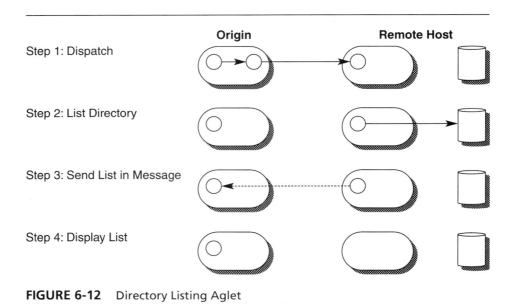

FIGURE 6-12   Directory Listing Aglet

this information. The message-based ListingAglet has two instance variables—
dir and proxy—which contain path information for the directory listing and
information about the message destination.

The aglet implements the onCreation method, which initializes the instance
variables from its init argument as given by the creator of the aglet. It also installs a mobility listener that handles the mobility event. When the aglet arrives
at the remote host, it will capture the directory listing (dir.list()) and will send
it with a message back to the creator at the origin (proxy.sendMessage()).

```
public class ListingAglet1 extends Aglet {
    File dir = null;
    AgletProxy proxy = null;

    public void onCreation(Object init) {
        dir = (File)((Object[])init)[0];
        proxy = (AgletProxy)((Object[])init)[1];

        addMobilityListener(
            new MobilityAdapter() {
                public void onArrival(MobilityEvent me) {
                    try {
                        proxy.sendMessage(new Message("Listing",
                                         dir.list()));
```

```
            } catch (Exception e) {
                dispose();
            }
        }
    }
    );
}
}
```

In the following code we show you how to create and set up the message-based `ListingAglet`. The creator can be, for example, a stationary aglet. In the first two lines, the destination and directory path are set. Then the current context, `context`, and the creator's proxy, `thisProxy`, are retrieved. The proxy is needed so that `ListingAglet` can send a message back to the creator. `Listing-Aglet` is created with the directory path and proxy information as initialization arguments. When the aglet has been created it is dispatched to the destination.

```
URL destination = new URL("atp://some.host.com");
File directory = new File("C:");
AgletContext context = getAgletContext();
AgletProxy thisProxy = getProxy();
Object[] init = new Object[] { directory, thisProxy };
AgletProxy proxy = context.createAglet(getCodeBase(),
                    "ListingAglet", init);
proxy.dispatch(destination);
```

The following message handler in the creator responds to `Listing` messages from `ListingAglet`. The argument carried by the message is of the `String[]` type and is listed by the handler.

```
public boolean handleMessage(Message msg) {
    if (msg.sameKind("Listing")) {
        String[] list = (String[])msg.getArg();
        for (int i = 0; i < list.length; )
            System.out.println(i + ": " + list[i++]);
        return true;      // Yes, I handled this message.
    } else
        return false;     // No, I did not handle this message.
}
```

6.9   Summary

In this chapter we taught you the basics of aglet messaging. Several means of interaglet communication were described. The first one was simple messaging with and without reply. This is the principal way for aglets to communicate with each other. Interaglet messaging is based on a simple event scheme that requires that an aglet implement handlers only for the kinds of messages that it is supposed to understand.

The second approach to interaglet communication is advanced message management. The message manager features a number of methods that enable the aglet to customize the behavior of the message manager. This set of methods includes the ability of the aglet to serialize messages, to prioritize messages by their kind, to allow parallel message handling, and to synchronize incoming messages.

Finally, we discussed multicast messaging between aglets. Message multicasting provides a powerful way for aglets to interact and collaborate. The basic principle is that aglets subscribe to one or more multicast messages and implement handlers for these messages.

In Chapter 7, we turn to the topic of aglet collaboration, covering the aglet proxy as well as aglet mobility and messaging in greater depth.

Chapter 7
Aglet Collaboration

No aglet is an island. Although aglets by nature are autonomous, they often need to act under some degree of control and, in particular, in collaboration with other aglets. Many complex tasks cannot be accomplished by a single aglet's work. For example, an aglet can receive services from other aglets by delegating specific tasks to specialized aglets. Mobility and messaging play important roles in collaboration, and in this chapter we will build on many of the techniques learned in the previous chapters.

We will first introduce the aglet proxy and describe the rationale behind this element of the Aglet API. This overview will be followed by a demonstration of different ways you can control aglets and make them collaborate. After reading this chapter you should be able to understand how the proxy works and how best to use it in your aglet programming to make aglets collaborate.

7.1 Aglet Proxy

An aglet is fundamentally a mobile event and message handler. Associated with each aglet is a proxy object that serves several purposes. Two of its most important roles are (1) as a shield to avoid uncontrolled access to the aglet's public methods and (2) as a convenient handle for a local, remote, or deactivated aglet (see Figure 7-1).

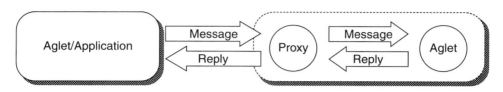

FIGURE 7-1   Relationship between Proxy and Aglet

When an aglet is created (`AgletContext.createAglet()`), it is automatically associated with a proxy object that is returned to the application. The application should then use this proxy to control the aglet. Unless the aglet gives away an object reference to itself, it is impossible for the application or any other aglet to access any of the public methods and fields in the aglet.

It should never be necessary to operate directly on the aglet itself. The application can control the aglet through the proxy's methods: `clone()`, `dispose()`, `dispatch()`, `deactivate()`, and `activate()`. The `clone` method will clone the aglet and return a proxy for the clone, `dispose()` will dispose of the aglet and invalidate its proxy, and `deactivate()` and `activate()` will maintain the proxy while deactivating and activating the aglet.

The `dispatch` method will return a new proxy that gives control of the remote aglet. It is here that location transparency comes in. The proxy returned by the `dispatch` method seems like any other proxy for a local aglet, but in fact it is what we call a *remote* proxy (see Figure 7-2). It allows the application to control the aglet through the proxy as if the aglet were local. As a consequence of this architecture, an aglet can have no more than one local proxy but multiple remote proxies. Notice that all of an aglet's proxies are invalidated when the aglet is either disposed of or dispatched.

Let us now describe each of the proxy's control methods in greater detail and show examples of how they work. The proxy's messaging methods were described in Chapter 6, so they will not be mentioned here.

7.1.1   Cloning

In Chapter 5 we demonstrated how an aglet could clone itself. Now we will show you how to clone an aglet through its proxy. The `AgletProxy` class features a `clone` method that, when invoked, will clone the aglet and return the proxy of the clone.

Public Object **AgletProxy.clone()**

Clones the proxy and the aglet that it holds. Notice that what is returned by this method is the cloned aglet proxy.

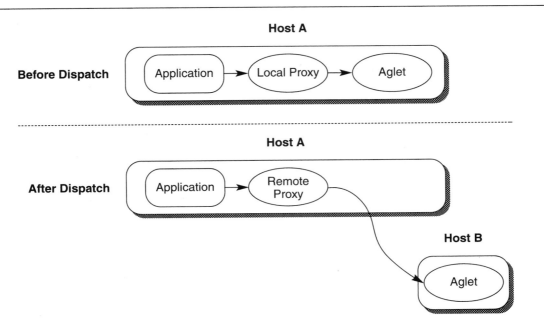

FIGURE 7-2   Location Transparency with the Proxy

ProxyCloneExample creates a child (ProxyCloneChild) and uses the child's
proxy to clone the child. It keeps both proxies—one for the child and one for the
clone—and uses them to demonstrate that the child and the clone have different
identities.

```
public class ProxyCloneExample extends Aglet {
   public void run() {
      try {
         AgletProxy proxy = getAgletContext().createAglet(
                               getCodeBase(), "ProxyCloneChild",
                               null);
         //Cloning the child.
         AgletProxy clonedProxy = (AgletProxy)proxy.clone();
         print("Original id: " + proxy.getAglet ID());
         print("Clone id:    " + clonedProxy.getAgletID());
      } catch (Exception e) {
         // Failed to create and clone the child.
      }
   }
}
```

7.1.2   Disposal

Unlike other Java objects, aglet objects are never garbage-collected automatically because an aglet is an active object with its own thread of control. However, one way to eliminate an aglet is by an invocation of the disposal method on the proxy (dispose()). Note that the aglet object will not be garbage-collected as long as one or more applications maintain local object references directly to the aglet.

When dispose() is invoked on the proxy, it disposes of the aglet and "cuts" the reference to it in order to facilitate garbage collection of the disposed-of aglet object. The proxy will not be garbage-collected as long it is referenced by the application. Therefore, when a proxy's aglet is disposed of, the proxy is marked invalid. The isValid method allows you to test the status of the aglet. The method returns false if the aglet has been disposed of; otherwise, it returns true. This works for both local and remote proxies.

public void **AgletProxy.dispose()**

Destroys and removes the aglet from its current aglet context. A successful invocation of this method will kill all threads created by the given aglet.

public boolean **AgletProxy.isValid()**

Tests whether the proxy is valid. Returns true if the proxy represents an existing aglet.

The ProxyDisposalExample aglet creates a child (ProxyDisposalChild) and confirms that the proxy of the child is valid before disposing of the child through the proxy. Afterward, it finds that the proxy has become invalid, because the aglet that it represents has been disposed of.

```
public class ProxyDisposalExample extends Aglet {
    public void run() {
        try {
            AgletProxy proxy = getAgletContext().createAglet(
                            getCodeBase(),
                            "ProxyDisposalChild",
                            null);
            print("Proxy Valid: "+proxy.isValid()); // Yes, it is.
            // Disposing of the child.
            proxy.dispose();
            print("Proxy Valid: "+proxy.isValid()); // Nope, it is not.
        } catch (Exception e) {
            // Failed to create and dispose of the child.
        }
    }
}
```

7.1.3   Dispatching

The proxy's dispatch method allows you to dispatch the aglet represented by the proxy. A successful invocation of the dispatch method will invalidate the proxy and will return a new proxy for the dispatched aglet. Another method, isRemote(), can be used to check whether the aglet represented by a given proxy is local to the proxy (in the same context) or remote.

public AgletProxy **AgletProxy.dispatch(URL destination)**

Dispatches the aglet to the location (host) specified by the destination argument.

public boolean **AgletProxy.isRemote()**

Tests whether the proxy represents a remote aglet.

The ProxyDispatchExample aglet creates a child (ProxyDispatchChild) and confirms that the proxy of the child is valid before dispatching the child to *destination*. Afterward, it finds that the proxy has become invalid, because the aglet that it represents has been dispatched. It also verifies that the new proxy returned by dispatch() is valid. The isRemote method is used to determine whether the aglet is local to the proxy (the result depends on *destination*).

```
public class ProxyDispatchExample extends Aglet {
    public void run() {
        try {
            AgletProxy proxy = getAgletContext().createAglet(
                                getCodeBase(),
                                "ProxyDispatchChild",
                                null);
            print("Proxy Valid:  " + proxy.isValid());
            print("Proxy Remote: " + proxy.isRemote());
            // Dispatching the child.
            AgletProxy remoteProxy = proxy.dispatch(destination);
            print("Proxy Valid:        " + proxy.isValid());
            print("Proxy Remote:       " + proxy.isRemote());
            print("Remote Proxy Valid:  " + remoteProxy.isValid());
            print("Remote Proxy Remote: " + remoteProxy.isRemote());
        } catch (Exception e) {
            // Failed to create and dispose of the child.
        }
    }
}
```

7.1.4 Deactivation and Activation

The proxy allows you to temporarily store an aglet in secondary storage (see Figure 7-3). When deactivating the aglet through its proxy, you need only specify how long the aglet should stay deactivated. By keeping a reference to the proxy object, your application can reactivate the aglet at any time (activate()). Use isActive() to test whether an aglet is active or in secondary storage.

Public void **AgletProxy.deactivate(long duration)**

Deactivates the aglet. The aglet will be temporarily stopped in its current context. It will resume execution after the specified period has elapsed.

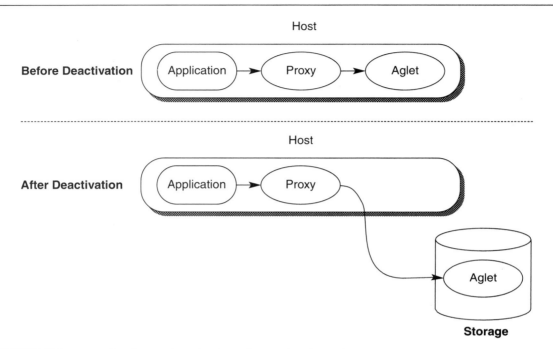

FIGURE 7-3   Deactivation and Activation of an Aglet through Its Proxy

Public void **AgletProxy.activate()**

Activates an aglet. This is a forced activation of a deactivated aglet.

Public boolean **AgletProxy.isActive()**

Tests whether the aglet has been deactivated. Returns true if the aglet is active or false if it has been deactivated.

Let us move on to an example. The ActivationExample aglet will first create a child (ActivationChild) and then will deactivate it for, say, 300 seconds. However, after a brief moment it changes its mind and explicitly activates the child aglet.

```
public class ActivationExample extends Aglet {

    public void run() {
        try {
            AgletProxy proxy = getAgletContext().createAglet(
                                getCodeBase(),
                                "agletbook.ActivationChild",
                                null);
```

```
                         try {
                            print(proxy.isActive() ? "Active" : "Not active");
                            // Should be 'Active'.
                            proxy.deactivate(300 * SECONDS);
                            print(proxy.isActive() ? "Active" : "Not active");
                            // Should be 'Not active'.
                            // Pause...
                            try {
                               proxy.activate;
                               print(proxy.isActive() ? "Active" : "Not active");
                               // Should be 'Active'.
                            } catch (Exception e) {
                               // Failed to activate the child.
                            }
                         } catch (Exception e) {
                            // Failed to deactivate the child.
                         }
                      } catch (Exception e) {
                         // Failed to create the child.
                         print(e.getMessage());
                      }
                   }
```

7.1.5 Aglet Information

Attached to each aglet is an information object, AgletInfo, which contains the following information about the aglet that it is attached to: identity, place of origin, time of creation, current location, class name, and code base. Use the proxy's getAgletInfo method to retrieve the AgletInfo object of an aglet.

public AgletInfo **AgletProxy.getAgletInfo()**
Gets the aglet's information object.

Use the following methods to retrieve the various attributes of the AgletInfo object.

public AgletID **AgletInfo.getAgletID()**
Gets the aglet's identity.

public String **AgletInfo.getAgletClassName()**
Gets the aglet's class name.

Public String **AgletInfo.getOrigin()**
Gets the origin address where the aglet was created.

public URL **AgletInfo.getCodeBase()**
Gets the aglet's code base.

public String **AgletInfo.getAddress()**
Gets the aglet's current location.

```
public long AgletInfo.getCreationTime()
```
Gets the aglet's time of creation.

The following quick example demonstrates how to retrieve information about the aglet from its proxy. The `ProxyInfoExample` aglet creates a child (`ProxyInfoChild`) and keeps the proxy of the child. It first gets the `AgletInfo` object from the proxy and then retrieves information such as the identifier, code base, class name, origin, current location, and time of creation.

```
public class ProxyInfoExample extends Aglet {
    public void run() {
        try {
            AgletProxy proxy = getAgletContext().createAglet(
                                    getCodeBase(), "ProxyInfoChild",
                                    null);
            AgletInfo info = proxy.getAgletInfo();
            print("Identifier: " + info.getAgletID());
            print("Code Base:  " + info.getCodeBase());
            print("Class Name: " + info.getAgletClassName());
            print("Origin:     " + info.getOrigin());
            print("Address:    " + info.getAddress());
            print("Creation:   " + new Date(info.getCreation-
                                    Time()));
        } catch (Exception e) {
            // Failed to create the child.
        }
    }
}
```

7.2   Controlling an Aglet

Now that we have introduced all the proxy's control methods it is time to demonstrate how they are used to make aglets collaborate. The example that we will look at has a parent aglet that lets its child roam and collect information while being kept on a short leash. In other words, the aglet's travel plan, the itinerary, remains at the origin with the parent aglet while the child aglet travels from host to host (see Figure 7-4).

The parent aglet is a stationary aglet that keeps the itinerary (`Controller-Example`) and a traveling aglet (`ControllerChild`). The itinerary is in the form of a list (`Vector`) of destinations. The key part of this example is the loop in the stationary aglet where the itinerary is traversed. For each destination element in the list, the traveling aglet is asked to dispatch via its proxy. Notice the way that the `proxy` variable is constantly updated in the body of the `while` loop: `proxy = proxy.dispatch(destination)`. Because the dispatch method is synchronous, you can safely assume that the proxy object must be valid. The method call does not return until the aglet has arrived at the new destination.

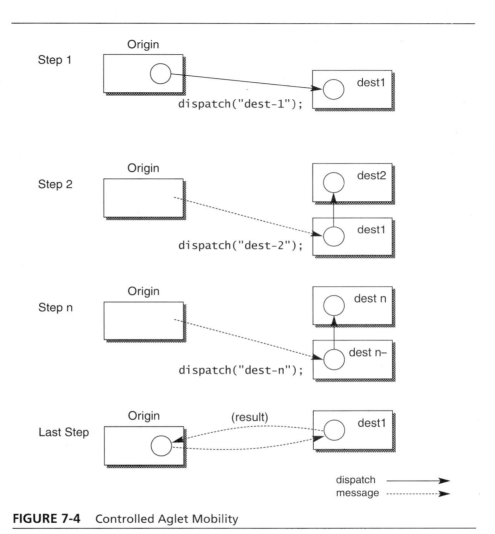

FIGURE 7-4 Controlled Aglet Mobility

```
public class ControllerExample extends Aglet {
    public void run() {
        try {
            AgletProxy proxy = getAgletContext().createAglet(
                            getCodeBase(),
                            "ControllerChild",
                            null);
            // Creates the travel itinerary.
            Vector itinerary = new Vector();
            itinerary.addElement(new URL(destination-1));
            itinerary.addElement(new URL(destination-2));
```

```
                    itinerary.addElement(new URL(destination-3));
                    itinerary.addElement(new URL(destination-n));
                    // Controls the travel of the child.
                    Enumeration enum = itinerary.elements();
                    while (enum.hasMoreElements())
                        proxy = proxy.dispatch((URL)enum.nextElement());
                } catch (Exception e) {
                    // Failed to create and dispose of the child.
                }
            }
        }
```

Notice that the `ControllerChild` aglet uses a `MobilityListener` to ensure the invocation of the generic method *doTask()* every time the traveling aglet arrives at a new location.

```
public class ControllerChild extends Aglet {
    public void onCreation(Object o) {
        addMobilityListener(
            new MobilityAdapter() {
                public void onArrival(MobilityEvent me) {
                    doTask();
                }
            }
        );
    }
    void doTask() {
        ...
    }
}
```

7.3 Finding an Aglet

The previous example demonstrated how one aglet could exercise full control over another aglet. We showed you the `ControllerExample` aglet, which always knows where `ControllerChild` is located. But what if the traveling aglet is autonomous? If it decides on its own where to go—perhaps based on information it gathers at each location it visits—how will other aglets be able to know where it currently is? There are many ways of locating an aglet. Here are three possibilities:

- *Search*. There are several ways to search for an aglet. One way is to send a search aglet to visit every host in the network to find the aglet you are looking for. Another way is to use multicasting and hope that the aglet in question will respond. Intuitively, this does not seem an efficient way to find aglets in a large network.

- *Logging*. Whenever an agent leaves a host, it leaves an electronic fingerprint that says where it is going. Hosts can transitively forward or redirect a request to a given aglet until it has been located. Note that logging imposes a penalty on remote messaging because of the forwarding of messages. Logging also consumes resources for maintaining a log on each server.

- *Registration.* Every aglet registers its current location in a database. This database always has the latest information available about an aglet's location. Note that registering the new location of an aglet adds overhead to the aglet's dispatch operation.

Aglet tracking is not supported in the Aglets API. A reliable forwarding mechanism is not easy to create at the application (aglet) level, but the registration approach can aptly be realized at the aglet level. Let us create an aglet tracking mechanism that permits the tracing of aglets registered with a stationary `AgletFinder`. The `AgletFinder` provides a mechanism for maintaining a dynamic name and location database of aglets, and it provides a way to locate aglets.

`AgletFinder` supports three kinds of messages:

- **Lookup: NAME.** The `Lookup` message returns the proxy of the specified aglet. An aglet can use this method to find another aglet with which it wants to communicate. The invoking agent specifies the demanded agent by symbolic name. `AgletFinder` cannot guarantee that an aglet will be in the location returned with the reply from this message. Note that the aglet can move after the `AgletFinder` has returned a location. There is also a potential source of false locations. Finally, a `Lookup` message can also reply with a proxy of an aglet that has been disposed of.

- **Register: NAME & PROXY.** The `Register` message adds the named aglet to the list of aglets registered with the `AgletFinder`. Because an aglet travels, this message may be sent many times by an aglet in its lifetime. If this message is sent by an aglet that already exists in the `AgletFinder`, this operation replaces the location information with the information in the most recent location.

- **Unregister: NAME.** The `Unregister` message removes the specified aglet from the list of aglets that are registered with the `AgletFinder`.

Figure 7-5 shows an example of two aglets that are using the `AgletFinder` to collaborate. The `Traveler` uses a mobility listener (`Register`) to register (1) with the `AgletFinder`. The `TravelerFinder` uses the `AgletFinder` to look up (2) the `Traveler` and sends it a message (3).

Now, we will guide you through the source code for the three aglets and the listener involved in this example: `AgletFinder`, `Traveler`, `TravelerFinder`, and `Register`.

The `AgletFinder` implements a simple database using a hash table (`Hashtable _database`). The database is maintained by the message handler (`handleMessage()`). The key-element pairs stored by the hash table are a symbolic name for the aglet and its proxy. `AgletFinder` responds to three kinds of messages: "Lookup" (`get(name)`), "Register" (`put(name, proxy)`), and "Unregister"

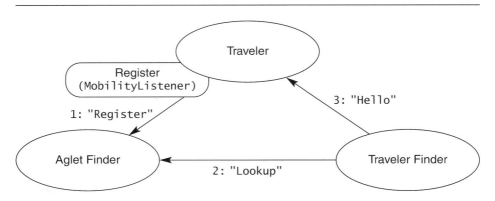

FIGURE 7-5   The AgletFinder Example

(remove(name)). Error handling is required but has been omitted for clarity. In particular, the "Lookup" and "Unregister" message handlers need to check the validity of the name argument. The onCreation method sets an "AgletFinder" property in the aglet context. This is a way to advertise its existence and its services to other aglets such as the Traveler aglet.

```
public class AgletFinder extends Aglet {
   // The aglet database.
   Hashtable _database = new Hashtable();
   // Advertises 'AgletFinder' in context properties.
   public void onCreation(Object init) {
      // Advertises its existence to other aglets.
      getAgletContext().setProperty("AgletFinder", getProxy());
   }
   // Handles messages.
   public boolean handleMessage(Message msg) {
      if (msg.sameKind("Lookup"))
         msg.sendReply(_database.get(msg.getArg()));
      else if (msg.sameKind("Register"))
         _database.put(msg.getArg("NAME"), msg.getArg("PROXY"));
      else if (msg.sameKind("Unregister"))
         _database.remove(msg.getArg("NAME"));
      return true;
   }
}
```

Now we'll describe an important reusable component of this example, the Register listener. Register extends the MobilityAdapter and overrides the onArrival method. Correctly set up, any aglet that this listener is plugged in to will automatically register with the AgletFinder whenever it arrives at a new destination. Register's constructor takes two arguments: a proxy reference to the AgletFinder and the symbolic name to register the aglet under. The onArrival method also invokes the generic *doTask* method. You are supposed to implement *doTask()* in the aglet. The listener also implements unregister(). This method will unregister the aglet with the AgletFinder.

```
public class Register extends MobilityAdapter {
    AgletProxy _finder;
    Message _msg = new Message("Register");
    // Initializes the listener.
    public Register(AgletProxy finder, String name) {
        _msg.setArg("NAME", name);
        _finder = finder;
    }
    // Registers the aglet on the arrival to a new host.
    public void onArrival(MobilityEvent me) {
        try {
            _msg.setArg("PROXY", me.getAgletProxy());
            _finder.sendMessage(_msg);
            doTask();
        } catch (Exception e) {
            // Failed to register.
        }
    }
    // Unregisters the aglet.
    public void unregister() {
        try {
            Message unregister = new Message("Unregister");
            unregister.setArg("NAME", _msg.getArg("NAME"));
            _finder.sendMessage(unregister);
        } catch (Exception e) {
            // Failed to unregister.
        }
    }
}
```

When the Traveler aglet is created, it first looks up the AgletFinder in its current context. Then it creates an instance of the reusable Register listener and plugs it in as its mobility listener. Now that the traveler is fully set up for traveling, it dispatches to its first destination. The implementation of its onDisposing method ensures that the aglet is unregistered from the AgletFinder when it is disposed of.

```
public class Traveler extends Aglet {
    Register _register = null;

    public void onCreation(Object o) {
        // Looks up the 'AgletFinder' in current context.
        AgletProxy finder = (AgletProxy)getAgletContext().getProperty(
            "AgletFinder"
        );
        // Initializes and plugs in the 'Register' listener.
```

```
            _register = new Register(finder, "Traveler");
            addMobilityListener(_register);
            // Starts traveling.
            try {
               dispatch(destination);
            } catch (Exception e) {
               // Failed to dispatch itself.
            }
         }
         // Unregisters when disposed of.
         public void onDisposing() {
            _register.unregister();
         }
         // Handles the 'Hello' message.
         public boolean handleMessage(Message msg) {
            if (msg.sameKind("Hello"))
               // Handles the 'hello' message.
            return true;
         }
      }
```

The task of the TravelerFinder aglet is to locate the Traveler and send a "Hello". First, the TravelerFinder looks up the AgletFinder in the current context (onCreation()). Then in the aglet's run method, it uses the AgletFinder to look up the aglet that has registered under the name "Traveler". The proxy object that is returned by the AgletFinder is then used to send a "Hello" message to the remote Traveler.

```
      public class TravelerFinder extends Aglet {
         AgletProxy _finder = null;

         public void onCreation(Object init) {
            // Looks up the 'AgletFinder' in current context.
            _finder = (AgletProxy)getAgletContext().
                         getProperty("AgletFinder");
         }

         public void run() {
            try {
               // Looks up the 'Traveler' and sends it a message.
               AgletProxy traveler = (AgletProxy)_finder.sendMessage(
                  new Message("Lookup", "Traveler")
               );
               traveler.sendMessage(new Message("Hello"));
            } catch (Exception e) {
               // Failed to send a message to 'Traveler'.
            }
         }
      }
```

The way to execute this example is first to start the AgletFinder and then the Traveler. When the Traveler has reached its destination you can start the TravelerFinder that will send a message to the Traveler.

7.4   Aglets in Parallel Execution

The last example in this chapter will demonstrate a way for an aglet to delegate its task to multiple aglets. For example, if an aglet must search 10 hosts for information it can do it either sequentially (the aglet visits all 10 hosts) or in parallel by creating 10 aglets (workers), each of which visits one host (see Figure 7-6).

The collaboration scheme for parallel execution is simple. The aglet creates a worker for each destination that is to be visited. The worker aglets are dispatched one by one to their respective destinations. Each worker implements the task (doTask()) that is executed by the message handler when it receives a "DoTask" message. Upon completion of a task, the worker returns its result as a reply to the parent aglet, which accumulates the incoming results. The workers self-destruct after having completed their mission.

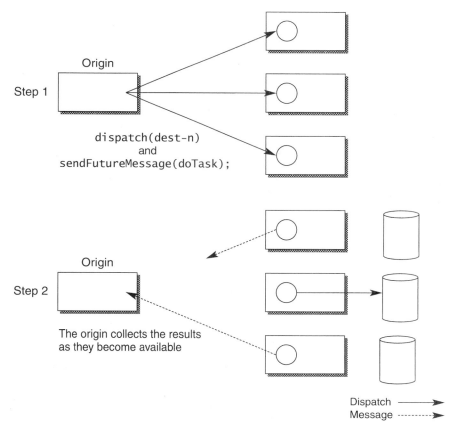

FIGURE 7-6   Parallel Execution of Aglets

```
public class Worker extends Aglet {
   public boolean handleMessage(Message msg) {
      if (msg.sameKind("DoTask"))
         msg.sendReply(doTask());
      dispose();
      return true;
   }
}
```

The parent aglet, ParallelExample, creates an itinerary (Vector) for all the destinations that are to be visited by workers. Then for each destination it creates a worker, dispatches it there, and sends it a future-based message. When all workers have been dispatched to their destinations, the parent aglet traverses all the replies and accumulates the results.

```
public class ParallelExample extends Aglet {
   public void onCreation(Object init) {
      // Creates the itinerary for parallel execution.
      Vector itinerary = new Vector();
      try {
         itinerary.addElement(new URL(destination-1));
         itinerary.addElement(new URL(destination-2));
         itinerary.addElement(new URL(destination-3));
         itinerary.addElement(new URL(destination-n));
      } catch (Exception e) {
         // Failed to create itinerary.
      }
      AgletContext context = getAgletContext();
      Message doTask = new Message("DoTask");
      ReplySet replies = new ReplySet();
      // Controls the travel of the workers.
      Enumeration enum = itinerary.elements();
      while (enum.hasMoreElements()) {
         try {
            AgletProxy worker = context.createAglet(
               getCodeBase(), "Worker", null);
            worker = worker.dispatch((URL)enum.nextElement());

      replies.addFutureReply(worker.sendFutureMessage(doTask));
         } catch (Exception e) {
            // Failed to dispatch.
         }
      }
      // Gets replies.
      while (replies.hasMoreFutureReplies()) {
         try {
            FutureReply future = replies.getNextFutureReply();
            accumulateResults(future.getResult());
         } catch (Exception e) {
            // Failed to receive replies.
         }
      }
   }
}
```

The two aglets that we just described collaborate in a *pull* mode. After the remote worker has arrived at its destination it will sit and wait for the parent aglet to send the "DoTask" message. Only then will it perform its doTask() and reply to the parent's message.

For completeness, let us show you an alternative implementation in which the aglets operate in a *push* mode. The worker now implements a mobility listener that invokes doTask() as soon as the aglet arrives at its destination. When doTask() returns, the aglet immediately sends a "Result" message to the parent aglet with the result of doTask() as an argument. The worker self-destructs when the message has been sent.

```
public class Worker1 extends Aglet {
    // Does the task and sends the result.
    public void onCreation(Object init) {
        AgletProxy parent = (AgletProxy)init;
        addMobilityListener(
          new MobilityAdapter() {
            public void onArrival(MobilityEvent me) {
              try {
                parent.sendMessage(new Message("Result",
                    doTask()));
                dispose();
              } catch (Exception e) {
                // Failed to send message with result.
              }
            }
          }
        );
    }
}
```

The parent aglet implements in the push variant a message handler that will receive and accumulate the result arguments of the incoming messages.

```
public class ParallelExample extends Aglet {
    public void onCreation(Object init) {
        // Creates the itinerary for parallel execution.
        Vector itinerary = new Vector();
        try {
            itinerary.addElement(new URL(destination-1));
            itinerary.addElement(new URL(destination-2));
            itinerary.addElement(new URL(destination-3));
            itinerary.addElement(new URL(destination-n));
        } catch (Exception e) {
            // Failed to create itinerary.
        }
        AgletContext context = getAgletContext();
        AgletProxy parent = getProxy();
        // Controls the travel of the workers.
        Enumeration enum = itinerary.elements();
        while (enum.hasMoreElements()) {
            try {
```

```
                    AgletProxy worker = context.createAglet(
                        getCodeBase(),
                        "Worker",
                        parent);
                    worker.dispatch((URL)enum.nextElement());
                } catch (Exception e) {
                    // Failed to dispatch.
                }
            }
        }
        // Handles the 'Result' messages.
        public boolean handleMessage(Message msg) {
            if (msg.sameKind("Result"))
                accumulateResults(msg.getArg());
            return true;
        }
    }
```

7.5   Summary

In this chapter we introduced the aglet proxy and demonstrated how it can be used to control the aglet for cloning, disposal, dispatching, and deactivation and activation. We then applied this controlling mechanism to aglet collaboration. In the controlled aglet example, we showed how a parent aglet could let its child roam and collect information while being kept on a short leash. We also gave an example of a more autonomous aglet that used an aglet finder utility to advertise its current location to other aglets. Our last example demonstrated a way for an aglet to delegate its task to multiple aglets that roam the network in parallel.

In Chapter 8, we will discuss how to use design patterns to streamline the task of implementing aglets in a variety of applications.

Chapter 8
Agent Design Patterns

In this chapter we will present several design patterns that we have found in agent-based applications. Weary of inventing and reinventing solutions to recurrent problems, we have found that agent design patterns can help by capturing solutions to common problems in agent design. We have also found that you need no unusual skills, language features, or other tricks to benefit from these patterns.

We expect agent design patterns to pragmatically fill the gap between high-level, agent-specific languages and system-level programming with the Aglet API. Patterns can also provide a sound foundation for visual development environments. We envision that the aglet developer can select and combine multiple patterns in a graphical environment. Based on standard implementations of these patterns, the development environment can generate aglets that have the desired properties.

Design patterns have proved highly useful within the object-oriented field and have helped developers to achieve good design of applications through reusability of validated components. We hope that the design patterns described in this chapter will serve this purpose in the context of aglet-based applications. It is not our intention to present an exhaustive catalog of agent design patterns. To cover this subject in depth would require an entire book. However, we hope that

Note: We would like to acknowledge Dr. Yariv Aridor of IBM Haifa Research Laboratory for his contribution to this chapter.

this chapter will motivate you to continue to discover more patterns that make it easier for designers of distributed applications to learn and use the Aglet API.

8.1   Classification of Agent Design Patterns

During the early work on the Aglet API, we recognized a number of recurrent patterns in the design of aglet applications. Several of these patterns were given intuitive, meaningful names such as *Master-Slave*, *Messenger*, and *Notifier*. They were implemented in Java and were included in the first release of the Aglets Workbench. These early patterns were found to be highly successful for jump-starting users who were new to aglets and the mobile agent paradigm.

This experience tells us that it is important to identify the elements of good reusable designs for aglet applications and to start formalizing developers' experience with these designs. This is the role of *design patterns*. The concept originated within the architectural community and was first formalized by software engineers and researchers in the object-oriented community. It has since been recognized as one of the most significant innovations in the object-oriented field.

The focus of this chapter is a new set of design patterns for creating aglet applications. We present a catalog of aglet designs and describe representative patterns. Our patterns have an object-oriented flavor, and we describe them by using the concepts of classes, objects, inheritance, and composition.

The patterns we have discovered so far can be divided into three classes: *traveling*, *task,* and *interaction*. This classification scheme makes it easier to understand the domain and application of each pattern, to distinguish different patterns, and to discover new patterns. We will briefly describe the three classes of patterns as well as the patterns in each class.

8.1.1   Traveling Patterns

Traveling is the essence of aglets. The traveling patterns deal with various aspects of managing the movements of aglets, such as routing and quality of service. These patterns allow us to enforce encapsulation of mobility management, which enhances reuse and simplifies aglet design.

The *Itinerary* pattern is an example of a traveling pattern that is concerned with routing among multiple destinations. An itinerary maintains a list of destinations, defines a routing scheme, handles special cases such as what to do if a destination does not exist, and always knows where to go next. Objectifying the itinerary allows you to save it and reuse it later in much the same way that you save URLs as bookmarks.

Another fundamental traveling pattern is the *Forward* pattern. This simple pattern allows a given host to mechanically forward all or specific aglets to another host.

The *Ticket* pattern, an enriched version of the concept of a URL, embodies requirements concerning quality of service, permissions, and other data. For example, it can include time-out information for dispatching an aglet to a remote host. Thus, instead of naively trying to dispatch to a disconnected host forever, the aglet now has the necessary information to make reasonable decisions while traveling.

8.1.2 Task Patterns

Task patterns are concerned with the breakdown of tasks and how these tasks are delegated to one or more aglets. In general, tasks can be dynamically assigned to general-purpose aglets. Furthermore, a given task can be accomplished either by a single aglet or by multiple aglets working in parallel and cooperating to accomplish it (such as in the case of a parallel search).

A fundamental task pattern is the *Master-Slave* pattern, which allows a master aglet to delegate a task to a slave aglet. The slave aglet moves to a destination host, performs the assigned task, and sends back the result of that task.

The more complex *Plan* pattern adopts a workflow concept to organize multiple tasks to be performed in sequence or in parallel by multiple aglets. The plan encapsulates the task flow, which is then hidden from the aglet. The aglet merely provides the mobility capabilities needed to perform activities at specific destinations. The plan promotes reusability of tasks, dynamic assignment of tasks to aglets, and even composition of tasks.

8.1.3 Interaction Patterns

The ability of aglets to communicate with one another is vital for cooperation among aglets. The interaction patterns are concerned with locating aglets and facilitating their interactions.

The *Meeting* pattern is an interaction pattern that provides a way for two or more aglets to initiate local interaction at a given host. It abstracts the synchronization in time and place that is required for local interactions. Aglets can dispatch themselves to a specific destination, called a *meeting place*, where they are notified of the arrival of their counterparts and can engage in local interaction.

Aglets can exploit the *Locker* pattern to temporarily store data in private. In this way, they can avoid bringing along data that for the moment are not needed. Later, aglets can return and retrieve the private data stored in the locker. For example, in an aglet-based purchasing system, an aglet may visit a vendor's host outside the company network. In this case, it can store its sensitive data in a locker before leaving the company network. The result is a reduction of network traffic and improved data confidentiality.

Aglets can establish remote communication by using the *Messenger* pattern, which objectifies messages in the form of aglets that carry and deliver messages between aglets. For example, if a slave aglet wishes to report a possibly interme-diate result back to the master aglet, it can send the result by a messenger aglet while continuing with its current task.

The *Finder* pattern describes a naming and locating service for aglets. It is often convenient to assign a symbolic (meaningful) name to an aglet in order to locate it later. For example, an information-gathering aglet may continuously move in the network and other aglets may from time to time wish to retrieve updates from the information-gathering aglet without actually knowing its present location.

Use the *Organized Group* pattern to compose multiple aglets into a group in which all members of the group travel together (we also call this the *group tour* pattern). This pattern can be considered a fundamental element of collaboration among multiple aglets.

The patterns are summarized in Table 8-1.

TABLE 8-1   Agent Design Patterns

Pattern	*Description*
TRAVELING PATTERNS	
Itinerary	Objectifies aglets' itineraries and routing among destinations.
Forwarding	Provides a way for a host to forward newly arrived aglets auto-matically to another host.
Ticket	Objectifies a destination address and encapsulates the quality of service and permissions needed to dispatch an aglet to a host address and execute it there.
TASK PATTERNS	
Master-Slave	Defines a scheme whereby a master aglet can delegate a task to a slave aglet.
Plan	Provides a way of defining the coordination of multiple tasks to be performed on multiple hosts.
INTERACTION PATTERNS	
Meeting	Provides a way for two or more aglets to initiate local interaction at a given host.
Locker	Defines a private storage space for data left by an aglet before it is temporarily dispatched (sent) to another destination.
Messenger	Defines a surrogate aglet to carry a remote message from one aglet to another.
Finder	Defines an aglet that provides services for naming and locating aglets with specific capabilities.
Organized Group	Composes aglets into groups in which all members of a group travel together.

8.2 The Master-Slave Pattern

Now let's look at the Master-Slave pattern in greater detail.

8.2.1 Definition

The Master-Slave pattern defines a scheme whereby a master aglet can delegate a task to a slave aglet.

8.2.2 Purpose

There are several reasons that some aglets—masters—would like to create other aglets—slaves—and delegate tasks to them. One reason is performance. A master aglet can continue to perform other tasks in parallel with the slave aglet. Another reason is illustrated via the following example. Consider an aglet-based application that provides a GUI for accepting data input and displaying the intermediate results of a specific task to be performed remotely. With a single aglet to provide the GUI and perform that task, it would not be possible to maintain the GUI (for example, to maintain an open window) after the aglet has traveled from its origin to a remote destination. Alternatively, a stationary master aglet can provide and maintain a GUI while a slave aglet moves to another destination, performs the assigned task, and delivers the task's result to the master aglet, which displays it to the client.

The key idea of the Master-Slave pattern is to use an abstract class, Slave, to localize the invariant parts of delegating a task between master and slave aglets: dispatching a slave to a remote destination, initiating the task's execution, and handling exceptions while performing the task. Concrete slave aglets are defined as subclasses of Slave, in which only varying parts, such as what task to perform, are implemented.

In practice, the master aglet defines a message handler that takes care of the task's result. The Slave class has two abstract methods—initializeTask and doTask—which define the initialization steps to be performed before the aglet travels to a new destination and the concrete task.

8.2.3 Applicability

Use the Master-Slave pattern in the following cases:

- When an aglet needs to perform a task in parallel with other tasks for which it is responsible
- When a stationary aglet wants to perform a task at a remote destination

Both cases concern tasks to be executed at a single destination.

8.2.4   Participants

Three classes participate in the Master-Slave pattern. See Figure 8-1 for their structural relationships.

- Slave defines a skeleton of a slave aglet, using abstract methods (initialize-Task and doTask) to be overridden in the ConcreteSlave class.
- ConcreteSlave implements the two abstract methods of the Slave class.
- Master implements the aglet that creates the slave aglet and receives the slave's result message.

8.2.5   Collaboration

The collaboration between the participants in the Master-Slave pattern is as follows (see also Figure 8-2):

1. A master aglet creates a slave aglet.
2. The slave initializes its task.

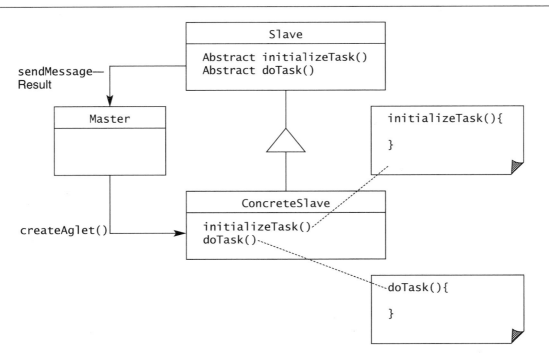

FIGURE 8-1   Participants in the Master-Slave Pattern

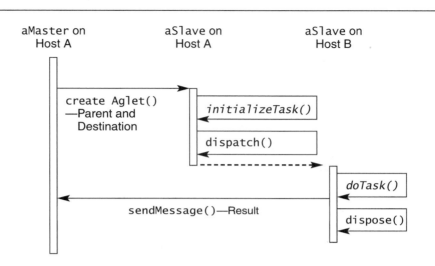

FIGURE 8-2   Collaboration in the Master-Slave Pattern

3. The slave moves to a remote host and performs its task.
4. The slave sends the result of the task to the master.
5. The slave disposes of itself.

8.2.6   Consequences

The Master-Slave pattern provides a fundamental way to reuse code among aglet classes. In practice, aglet design and implementation are simplified by letting developers implement only the variable aspects of predefined patterns.

One drawback of an inheritance-based pattern is that the behavior of a slave aglet is fixed at design time. For example, an aglet cannot be transformed into a slave at runtime, nor can a slave aglet easily be assigned to perform new tasks. A more sophisticated version of this pattern can use a delegation-based model, in which the task is objectified and a slave aglet can be assigned any task object during its lifetime.

8.2.7   Implementation

Let us describe an implementation of a generic slave aglet based on the Master-Slave pattern. First, we will describe the reusable Slave class, and then we will demonstrate the use of the class with a simple example.

The abstract Slave class implements the onCreation method that performs the necessary initialization of the slave. It also defines two abstract *methods—*

initializeTask and *doTask*—that are supposed to be overridden by the concrete slave class. The onCreation method takes an object argument that contains the necessary information for the slave aglet to function properly: *destination* information so that the slave knows where to go, and a reference to the *master* aglet so that the slave can send back the result of its work.

When created, the slave aglet will invoke *initializeTask()*, followed by a dispatch to the specified location. When it arrives at the destination, it invokes *doTask()* and sends back the result returned by this method to the specified master aglet. Having accomplished its mission, it destroys itself.

```
public abstract class Slave extends Aglet {
    // The setup of the slave (Master and Destination).
    URL destination = null;
    AgletProxy master = null;

    public void onCreation(Object args) {
        try {
            // Gets the setup.
            destination = (URL)((Object[])args)[0];
            master = (AgletProxy)((Object[])args)[1];
            initializeTask();
            addMobilityListener(
                new MobilityAdapter() {
                    public void onArrival(MobilityEvent me) {
                    try {
                        master.sendMessage(new Message(
                        "Result", doTask()));
                        dispose();
                    } catch (Exception e) {
                        // Failed to send result to master.
                    }
                    }
                }
            );
            dispatch(destination);
        } catch (Exception e) {
            // Failed to create slave.
        }
    }
    // 'initializeTask' to be implemented in subclass.
    abstract void initializeTask();
    // 'doTask' to be implemented in subclass.
    abstract Object doTask();
}
```

Now let us present two aglets—MyMaster and MySlave—that play the script outlined by the Master-Slave pattern. MyMaster first creates the initialization arguments for the slave that contains destination information and a reference to the master's proxy. Then the concrete slave aglet, MySlave, is created. All the master aglet now must do is to wait for the slave aglet to return a result message when it has completed its task.

```
public class MyMaster extends Aglet {
    // Creates the slave aglet.
    public void run() {
        try {
            Object[] args = new Object[] {
                    destination,
                    getAgletProxy() };
                    getAgletContext().createAglet(
                    getCodeBase(),
                    "MySlave",
                    args);
        } catch (Exception e) {
            // Failed to create the child.
        }
    }
    // Handles the slave's result message.
    public boolean handleMessage(Message msg) {
        if (msg.sameKind("Result"))
            // Processes 'msg.getArg()' here.
        return true;
    }
}
```

The MySlave class extends the abstract Slave class. The only requirement for MySlave is to implement the Slave's two abstract methods: *initializeTask* and *doTask*. Notice the rudimentary character of this class. The entire focus of the programmer will be on the variable aspects, that is, the implementation of the two abstract methods.

```
public class MySlave extends Slave {
    // Concrete initialization method.
    public void initializeTask() {
        print("Initializing.");
    }
    // Concrete task method.
    public Object doTask() {
        // Performs some task...
        return result;
    }
}
```

8.3   The Itinerary Pattern

Now let's look at the Itinerary pattern in some detail.

8.3.1   Definition

The Itinerary pattern objectifies aglets' itineraries and their navigation among multiple destinations.

8.3.2   Purpose

Being an autonomous mobile entity, an itinerary-based aglet can navigate independently to multiple hosts. Specifically, it should be able to handle exceptions such as unknown hosts while trying to dispatch itself to new destinations. It might even need to modify its itinerary dynamically depending on local information. For example, it might dispatch itself to inquire about a local Yellow Pages service, extract relevant destinations, and add them on-the-fly to its itinerary.

The key idea of this pattern is to shift the responsibility for navigation from the aglet to its associated `Itinerary` object. The `Itinerary` class will provide an interface to maintain or modify the aglet's itinerary and to dispatch the aglet to new destinations. An aglet object and an `Itinerary` object will be connected as follows. The aglet will create the `Itinerary` object and initialize it with (1) a list of destinations to be visited sequentially and (2) a reference to the aglet. Then the aglet will use the go method to dispatch itself to the next available destination in its itinerary. To support this, it is necessary that the `Itinerary` object be transferred together with the aglet.

8.3.3   Applicability

Use this pattern when you wish to do the following:

- Hide the specifics of an aglet's travel plan from its behavior to promote modularity of both parts
- Provide a uniform interface for the traveling of aglets
- Define travel plans that can be reused and shared by aglets

8.3.4   Participants

Figure 8-3 shows the structural relationships among the participants of this pattern.

- `Itinerary` defines a skeleton of an itinerary, with two abstract methods: go and hasMoreDestinations.
- `ConcreteItinerary` implements the abstract methods of the `Itinerary` class and keeps track of the current destination of the aglet.
- `Aglet` is the `Aglet` base class.

8.3.5   Collaboration

Figure 8-4 shows collaboration according to this pattern:

1. The `ConcreteItinerary` object is initialized by the aglet.
2. The `ConcreteItinerary` dispatches the aglet to the first destination.

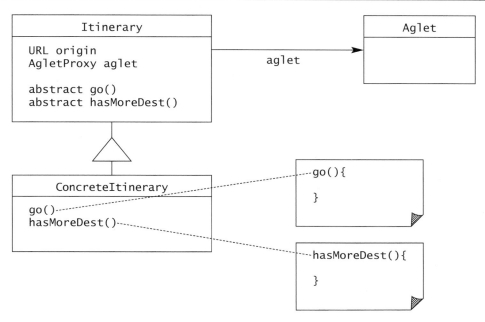

FIGURE 8-3 Participants in the Itinerary Pattern

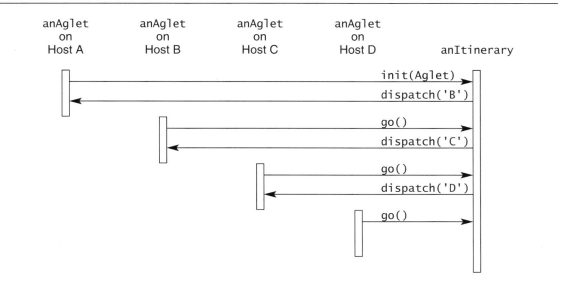

FIGURE 8-4 Collaboration in the Itinerary Pattern

3. When the aglet invokes the itinerary's go method, the aglet is dispatched to the next destination.

8.3.6 Consequences

This pattern supports variations in navigation. For example, a different exception-handling routine can be defined if an aglet fails to dispatch itself to a new destination: cancel the trip and return to the origin, try to go to another destination, and later try again. This pattern makes it easy to provide such variations by simply replacing one Itinerary object with another one. Most important, it will not require the aglet class to be modified. This pattern also facilitates sharing of travel plans by different aglets. For example, two aglets can use the same tour to multiple users' desktops: one to schedule a meeting between all users and the other to deliver them notification messages.

8.3.7 Implementation

Now we will present an implementation of an abstract Itinerary class based on the Itinerary pattern. We will also show an example of a concrete itinerary and an itinerant aglet based on this class and pattern.

The Itinerary class has a constructor that sets the origin, one of the itinerary's two fields. The other field, aglet, is set by the init() method. This method also dispatches the aglet to its first destination. The Itinerary class defines three abstract methods: go, hasMoreDestinations, and getNextDestination. Each of these methods is supposed to be implemented in the concrete itinerary classes.

```
public abstract class Itinerary implements Serializable {
    protected URL _origin = null;
    protected AgletProxy _aglet = null;
    // Constructs the itinerary with information of origin.
    public Itinerary(URL origin) {
        _origin = origin;
    }
    // Initializes the itinerary with a reference to the itinerant
            aglet.
    public void init(Aglet aglet) {
        _aglet = aglet.getAgletContext().getAgletProxy(
                aglet.getAgletID());
        go();
    }
    // Gets the origin information.
    public URL getOrigin() {
        return _origin;
    }
    // Makes the itinerant aglet dispatch to the specified location.
    protected void go(URL destination) throws Exception {
        _aglet.dispatch(destination);
    }
```

```
            // 'go()' to be implemented in subclass.
            public abstract void go();
            // 'hasMoreDestinations()' to be implemented in subclass.
            public abstract boolean hasMoreDestinations();
            // 'getNextDestination()' to be implemented in subclass.
            public abstract URL getNextDestination();
        }
```

Based on the generic Itinerary class, we have created an itinerant aglet, ItinerantAglet, that given any concrete itinerary will follow the dictated travel plan autonomously. This aglet implements the onCreation method, which takes the itinerary as its argument. The onCreation method initializes the itinerary (init()). It also instantiates a mobility listener that invokes the itinerary's go method every time the aglet arrives at a new destination. If the itinerary has no more destinations, the aglet will dispose of itself.

```
        public class ItinerantAglet extends Aglet {
            private Itinerary _itinerary = null;
            public void onCreation(Object init) {
                try {
                    _itinerary = (Itinerary)init;
                    addMobilityListener(
                        new MobilityAdapter() {
                            public void onArrival(MobilityEvent me) {
                                try {
                                    if (_itinerary.hasMoreDestinations()) {
                                        // Goes to next destination...
                                        _itinerary.go();
                                    } else {
                                        // Done...
                                        dispose();
                                    }
                                } catch (Exception e) {
                                    // Failed to dispatch.
                                }
                            }
                        }
                    );
                    // Goes to first destination.
                    _itinerary.init(this);
                } catch (Exception e) {
                    // Failed to initialize the itinerary.
                }
            }
        }
```

Let us continue with a simple but useful concrete itinerary called the sequential itinerary, SeqItinerary. This itinerary is essentially an ordered list of destinations that the itinerant aglet will visit one by one. SeqItinerary's constructor takes the origin and a Vector of destinations as initial arguments. The go() is implemented; it will traverse the Vector from first to last element. Destinations to which it fails to dispatch will simply be skipped.

```
public class SeqItinerary extends Itinerary {
   private Vector _destinations = null;
   // Constructs the itinerary with origin and destination
      information.
   SeqItinerary(URL origin, Vector destinations) {
      super(origin);
      _destinations = (Vector)destinations.clone();
   }
   // Dispatches the itinerant aglet to the next destination.
   public void go() {
      URL dest = getNextDestination();
      if (dest != null) {
         _destinations.removeElementAt(0);
         try {
            go(dest);
         } catch (Exception e) {
            // Failed to dispatch.
            // Skip this destination and go for the next.
            go();
         }
      }
   }
   // Returns the number of remaining destinations.
   public boolean hasMoreDestinations() {
      return _destinations.size() > 0;
   }
   // Returns the next destination.
   public URL getNextDestination() {
      if (hasMoreDestinations())
         return (URL)_destinations.firstElement();
      else
         return null;
   }
}
```

The final element in this example is the aglet that binds it all together:
Parent. This aglet creates and initializes the concrete itinerary, SeqItinerary,
and hands it over to the itinerant aglet, ItinerantAglet. The itinerant aglet
autonomously follows the travel plan and visits the places dictated by the specified itinerary.

```
public class Parent extends Aglet {
   Itinerary _itinerary = null;
   public void onCreation(Object init) {
      try {
         Vector destinations = new Vector();
         destinations.addElement(destination-1);
         destinations.addElement(destination-2);
         destinations.addElement(destination-3);
         destinations.addElement(destination-n);
         URL origin = getAgletContext().getHostingURL();
```

```
                    getAgletContext().createAglet(getCodeBase(),
                                              "ItinerantAglet",
                              new SeqItinerary(origin,
                              destinations));
            } catch (Exception e) {
              // Failed to initialize the itinerary.
            }
        }
    }
```

8.4 Master-Slave Revisited

Let us return for a moment to the Master-Slave pattern. So far we have described only slaves that have fairly simple single-destination travel plans. The slave aglet dispatches to a remote host, performs its task, and returns the result. Why not incorporate the Itinerary pattern into the Master-Slave pattern?

Not surprisingly, the result is a slave aglet that travels according to its itinerary. It visits multiple hosts, and executes its task on each host (*doTask()*). Figure 8-5 shows a collaboration diagram for the master aglet and its itinerant slave aglet.

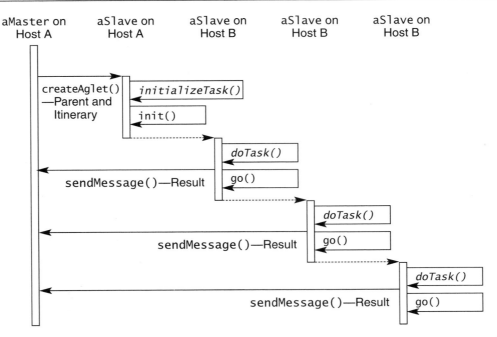

FIGURE 8-5 The Itinerary-Based Slave Aglet

The implementation of the new Slave class is similar to that of the original one. The key additions are the initialization of the itinerary (init()) in the aglet's onCreation method and the addition of go() in the mobility listener's onArrival method. Every time the aglet arrives at a new location, it executes *doTask()* and sends back the result to the master. Then it consults with the itinerary to see whether there are more destinations to visit or it has completed the trip and can dispose of itself.

```java
public abstract class Slave extends Aglet {
    Itinerary itinerary = null;
    AgletProxy parent = null;

    public void onCreation(Object args) {
        try {
            itinerary = (Itinerary)((Object[])args)[0];
            parent = (AgletProxy)((Object[])args)[1];
            initializeTask();
            addMobilityListener(
                new MobilityAdapter() {
                    public void onArrival(MobilityEvent me) {
                    try {
                        parent.sendMessage(new Message("Result",
                            doTask()));
                        if (itinerary.hasMoreDestinations())
                            // Goes to next destination.
                            itinerary.go();
                        else
                            // Done...
                            dispose();
                    } catch (Exception e) {
                        // Failed to send result to master.
                    }
                }
            );
            itinerary.init(this);
        } catch (Exception e) {
            // Failed to create slave.
        }
    }
    abstract void initializeTask();
    abstract Object doTask();
}
```

In this example, we let the master aglet create an instance of the previously introduced SeqItinerary class. This itinerary will provide the slave aglet with a simple travel plan in which the slave's *doTask()* is executed at each destination.

```java
public class MyMaster extends Aglet {
    public void run() {
        try {
            Vector destinations = new Vector();
            destinations.addElement(destination-1);
```

```
                    destinations.addElement(destination-2);
                    destinations.addElement(destination-3);
                    destinations.addElement(destination-n);
                    URL origin = getAgletContext().getHostingURL();
                    SeqItinerary itinerary = new SeqItinerary(origin,
                                            destinations);
                    AgletProxy thisProxy = getAgletContext().
                        getAgletProxy(getAgletID());
                    Object[] args = new Object[] { itinerary, thisProxy };
                                    getAgletContext().
                                    createAglet(getCodeBase(),
                                    "MySlave", args);
            } catch (Exception e) {
                // Failed to create the child.
            }
        }
    }
```

8.5   Summary

In this chapter we have reported on several design patterns that we have found in aglet applications. Weary of inventing and reinventing solutions to recurrent problems, we have found that agent design patterns can help by capturing solutions to common problems in agent design. You need no special skills, language features, or other tricks to benefit from these patterns.

We expect agent patterns to pragmatically fill the gap between high-level, agent-specific languages and system-level programming languages such as Java. Patterns can also provide a sound foundation for visual agent development environments. We envision that the agent developer can select and combine multiple patterns in a graphical environment. Based on standard implementations of these patterns, the development environment can generate agents having the desired properties. Design patterns have proved to be highly useful within the object-oriented field and have helped developers to achieve good design of applications through reusability of validated components. We hope that the design patterns described in this chapter and the catalog will serve this purpose in the context of mobile agent-based applications.

Chapter 9 examines the inner workings of aglets, taking a close look at the Aglets framework.

Chapter 9
Inside Aglets

In most cases, the classes and methods of the Aglet API are all you need to know about to program an aglet. But in rare situations, or perhaps from pure curiosity, you may want to know what is under the hood. You may already understand that the Aglet API is the thin outer shell of a much bigger system called the *Aglets framework*. The Aglet API is implemented in the Aglets runtime layer, which in turn is based on the communication layer.

It is not the purpose of this chapter to describe *how* the Aglets framework is implemented. After all, you do not have to know much about combustion engines to drive a car. On the other hand, even a minuscule knowledge of the inner workings may in certain cases vastly improve your performance. With that in mind we have carefully selected parts of the Aglets framework for a closer presentation along with a general overview of the framework's components.

After reading this chapter you should have a sufficient understanding of the inner workings of the Aglets framework to optimize the performance of your aglets, to understand why apparently healthy aglets are malfunctioning, and to make better overall use of the Aglet API in your programming.

9.1 Architectural Overview

The Aglets framework consists of three layers. On the top is the application layer with the user-defined aglets. These aglets interface with the Aglet API and its implementation, the Aglets runtime layer. At the bottom is the Communication API and its implementation. Figure 9-1 shows the structure of the Aglets framework.

The Aglets runtime layer, needed for the proper management and execution of aglets, consists of two parts: a core framework and a set of extensible system management components. We'll describe each of these parts separately and then briefly describe the communication layer.

9.1.1   Core Framework

In reality, it is the core framework that implements the Aglet API. This framework provides the core services necessary for executing aglets, including basic operations such as creation, cloning, dispatching, retraction, deactivation, and activation. The primary functions of the core framework are to securely manage the following:

- Initialization and serialization/deserialization of aglets
- Class loading and transfer
- Aglet references and garbage collection

We will cover these functions in greater detail later in the chapter.

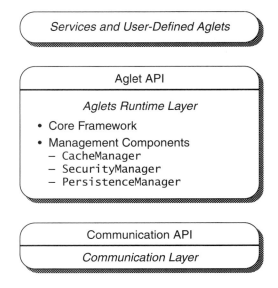

FIGURE 9-1   The Aglets Framework

9.1.2 Management Components

The Aglets runtime layer also features the following components, which are designed to be customizable, albeit not by the aglet programmer. They are intended for the creator of an aglet server and can conveniently be used to optimize and tailor the performance and security of a given server.

- The *PersistenceManager* component is responsible for storing and retrieving deactivated (serialized) aglets. The PersistenceManager stores the byte code and state of a deactivated aglet in secondary storage. Depending on the actual implementation of the PersistenceManager, it may use anything from a database to the raw file system to store persistent aglets. The current implementation of Aglets (at the time of writing) stores aglets in the file system.

- The *CacheManager* component is responsible for managing byte code and other resources, such as images, used by aglets. Because aglet byte code needs to be transferred when an aglet moves between servers, the cache mechanisms can help to improve the performance of agent transfer.

- The *SecurityManager* component is responsible for protecting hosts and aglets from malicious entities. Every security-sensitive operation requires consultation with the security manager to check whether the given aglet is actually permitted to perform the requested operation. The SecurityManager component is based on the Java language system's SecurityManager class.

The management components are defined as either interfaces or abstract classes and can thus be implemented or extended to fit the specific environment in which a given aglet server is deployed. For example, the implementation of SecurityManager will depend on the particular security policy in play. And that policy will very much depend on whether the aglet server is running in a closed network in a manufacturing facility or is directly connected to the Internet.

The APIs for the management components are generally not of interest to the aglet programmer. However, understanding the behavior of these components on specific aglet servers may be a key to understanding the capabilities and limitations of aglets. The CacheManager component may cache aglet byte code in a way that makes it difficult to control the propagation of aglet class updates (versions) throughout the network, and a restrictive SecurityManager component may severely limit an aglet's ability to access local resources at a given server.

9.1.3 Communication Layer

The Aglets runtime layer has no built-in mechanism for transporting aglets over the network. Instead, the Aglets runtime layer interfaces with the generic communication layer. This API and its implementation constitute an *agent* transport and communication mechanism independent of Aglets. The separation of the Aglets runtime implementation and the transport mechanism means that Aglets does not rely on a single kind of transport mechanism.

The current implementation of the communication layer uses the Agent Transfer Protocol. ATP is an application-level Internet protocol modeled on the HTTP protocol and is used to transport mobile agents as well as to provide remote messaging for agents. This layer is discussed in greater detail later in the chapter.

9.2   Aglet Object Structure

Now that we have had a high-level view of the Aglets framework, it is time to zoom in on the microstructure that surrounds the individual aglet. In the center of this structure we find an instance of the `AgletRef` object, a composite object that consists of several components in addition to the aglet object itself. The `AgletRef` object is inside the framework and not available to aglet programmers. The aglet object structure is shown in Figure 9-2.

You can consider `AgletRef` to be the true implementation of the somewhat shallow `Aglet` class. `AgletRef` implements the key functions of the aglet, including dispatching, retraction, and cloning; invocations of several methods on an `Aglet` object are actually forwarded to the `AgletRef` object. This object also maintains aglet properties such as identity and address.

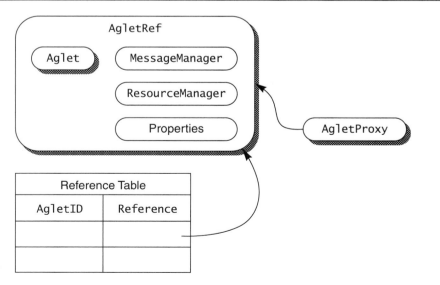

FIGURE 9-2   Structure of an Aglet Object

The `AgletRef` object is a reference object that is stored in the framework's *aglet reference table*, the table that is used to look up aglets. The application layer's reference objects—namely, the `AgletProxy` objects—also provide indirection by not referring to the aglet directly. Instead, they contain references to the `AgletRef` object. Notice that multiple proxy objects can refer to the same `AgletRef` object.

Unlike other Java objects, aglets are never garbage-collected automatically, because an aglet is an active object (an agent) that has its own thread of execution. When an aglet has been dispatched, deactivated, or disposed of, the connection between that aglet and the reference object is cut off so that the Java language system's automatic garbage collector can sweep up the dangling objects. This means that if you keep a reference to an aglet elsewhere, it will not be garbage-collected. For example, if you have a reference to the static variable of the class, it will not be garbage-collected.

```
public MyAglet extends Aglet {
    static MyAglet aglet = null;
    public void onCreation(Object init) {
        // Maintains a static reference to itself.
        // Avoids the garbage collector.
        aglet = this;
    }
}
```

Note that a reference object may not be garbage-collected immediately even if its embedded aglet has been disposed of and the reference object itself has been removed from the reference table. The simple explanation is that other aglets may still have proxy objects that refer to that particular reference object, thus keeping it "alive."

Let us briefly turn to some of the other objects embedded by the `AgletRef` object, namely the `MessageManager` and `ResourceManager` components:

- The *MessageManager* component is responsible for managing incoming messages and events. All messages and events are first passed to the `MessageManager`, which functions as a monitor for the aglet. If the monitor is not occupied, the message will be forwarded to the aglet; otherwise, it will be queued for later processing. Note that aglet events are also in the sphere of the `MessageManager` and that events and messages are therefore handled in a uniform way.

- The *ResourceManager* component is responsible for managing the resources accessed, allocated, and consumed by the aglet. For example, the `ResourceManager` component automatically disposes of windows opened by an aglet when the aglet is disposed of, dispatched, or deactivated. Although it should be possible to manage all resources consumed by an aglet, there are certain limitations. Currently, the `ResourceManager` component supports only window and thread management. Control of resources related to the file system (such as open files) or the network (such as open sockets) is not supported at the time of writing. Thus, aglet programmers must manage these resources manually or risk wasting them.

9.3   Initialization and Serialization of Aglets

So far we have focused on the structural aspects of the Aglets framework. In this section, we will cover some details of the initialization and serialization of aglets.

9.3.1   Initialization of Aglets

When you create an aglet, the Aglets framework performs the following steps:

1. Locate the aglet class, load the class data, and define a new class (if it is not already defined). In Java, to define a class means to turn an array of bytes into an instance of the class `Class`.
2. Instantiate a new object from that class (execute the constructor).
3. Create the reference object (`AgletRef`) and establish the aglet connection.
4. Start the aglet's execution.

Notice that the connection between the reference object and the aglet is not created until after the execution of the aglet's constructor is complete. The implication is that the aglet cannot access any methods of the `Aglet` class from its constructor.

```
public MyAglet extends Aglet implement Externalizable {
    int i=0;
    public MyAglet() {
        getAgletContext();   // Will not work!
        i++;                 // Also when the aglet is deserialized.
    }
}
```

Note that the constructor with no arguments is called every time the aglet that implements `java.io.Externalizable` is deserialized. In the preceding example, the counter i will be incremented every time the aglet is deserialized. This follows from the specification of the Java serialization mechanism and cannot be avoided. As a consequence, we recommend that you avoid using the aglet's constructor to initialize an aglet.

Let us take a look at class (static) variables in your aglet classes. The initialization of class variables takes place only once per class and happens at the same time as the instantiation of the first object of that class. The initialization of class variables is performed in the context of that aglet. This means that the same security restrictions apply to the initialization process as do those of the given aglet.

In the following example, we let an aglet class automatically instantiate two class variables: `myDialog` and `myThread`. When the aglet starts executing, it can expect that both variables have been properly initialized. As is customary, the onDisposing method is designed to release the aglet's resources (myDialog and myThread) when it is disposed of.

```
public class MyAglet extends Aglet {
    static MyDialog myDialog = new MyDialog();
    static Thread myThread = new Thread();

    public void onDisposing() {
        // Releases its resources.
        myDialog.dispose();
        myThread.stop();
    }
}
```

However, because the same class may later be reused to instantiate yet another aglet, this new aglet may fail to work properly, because none of the class variables has been initialized. The lesson here is that class variables should be considered resources that are shared among all instances of the given class, and they should be used with extraordinary caution.

9.3.2 Serialization and Object Mobility

When you dispatch, deactivate, or clone an aglet, serialization of the aglet takes place. Serialization begins with the aglet object and traverses all reachable objects except for transient references. In addition, the properties of the aglet, such as user information, origin address, and byte code of classes used in the aglet, are placed in a byte array. This array is then either used to create a clone, handed over to the PersistenceManager, or passed to the communication layer.

The Aglets framework uses a standard Java object serialization mechanism to marshal and unmarshal the state of aglets into a stream. During serialization, all nontransient objects that are reachable from the aglet object are regarded as its state and are visited for marshaling. Therefore, all objects that need to be transferred should be nontransient and should implement the java.io.Serializable interface or the java.io.Externalizable interface to be successfully serialized. If a nonserializable object is found in the object graph, an exception, java.io.NotSerializableException, will be thrown.

```
class MyAglet extends Aglet {
    // Vector class is serializable and will be transferred.
    private Vector result = new Vector();
    // Transient variable 'in' will not be serialized and transferred
    transient InputStream in = new InputStream();
}
```

Note that objects handled in a serialization/deserialization process are stored *by value*. That is, once serialized, an object shared by multiple aglets is *copied* and is no longer shared after a dispatching, cloning, and deactivation/ activation operation.

However, when an `AgletProxy` object is transferred it keeps the aglet identity and its address, using that information to restore the correct reference to the original aglet. Therefore, `AgletProxy` objects can keep the reference to the actual aglet even if the proxy is transferred to a remote host or deactivated, as long as the aglet remains in the same location.

```
class Transferrable implements java.io.Serializable {
    Hashtable hash;
}
class NonTransferrable {
    int dummy;
}
class MyAglet extends Aglet {
    transient FileDescriptor fd; // Do not transfer.
    int value;
    String str;
    AgletProxy proxy;
    Object transferrable = null;
    Object not_transferrable = null;
    public void onCreation(Object init) {
        transferrable = new Transferrable();
        // Transfer by value. not_transferrable = new NonTransferrable();
        // Will fail to transfer.
    }
}
```

Because class variables are not a part of the object, their values are never serialized or transferred. Thus, the class variables are local to that class, and the aglet may retrieve a different value when it arrives at the new destination and accesses a given class variable.

```
public class MyAglet {
    // A class variable.
    static int classVariable = 0;
    // Dispatches the aglet.
    public void onCreation(Object init) {
        try {
        classVariable = 10;
        dispatch(new URL("atp://next.place"));
        } catch(Exception ex) {
            ...
        }
    }
    // Gets different values from 'classVariable'.
    public void run() {
        if (classVariable != 10) {
            System.out.println("Class variables never get
                            transferred!");
        }
    }
}
```

Object serialization provides two ways of customizing serialization for an object of a given class. The first way to customize serialization for a given class is to implement two methods—writeObject and readObject, of the java.io. Serializable interface. The second way is to implement writeExternal() and readExternal()—of the java.io.Externalizable interface. The purpose of the Externalizable interface is to allow you to customize the *way* in which a given state is serialized and deserialized. You may want to consult with the Java language system's object serialization specification for further details on these matters.

It is important to understand that readObject() and readExternal() are called in the process of serialization. That is, these two methods are called before the aglet is properly established with its reference object in the Aglets framework. Like the aglet's constructor, the implementations of these methods cannot use any of the methods of the Aglet class. Similarly, writeObject() and write-External() are called after the aglet is suspended and invalidated.

9.4   Class Loading and Transfer

In mobile agent systems, classes for an agent need to be available at the server where the agent is supposed to execute. Consequently, mobile agent systems must either load byte code on demand or else transfer the byte code along with the agent. The Aglets framework combines these two schemes to transfer byte code in the most flexible way. It also uses a byte code cache to reduce unnecessary downloading of classes. In this section we will cover class loading, class transfer, and class resumption and evolution.

9.4.1   Class Loading

In the Aglets framework, the classes an aglet needs for creation and execution are determined at runtime—that is, classes for the aglet are loaded dynamically and on demand. Dynamic class loading may also happen later in the life of an aglet while it is visiting remote hosts.

In the Java language system, there is a special class, ClassLoader, that is capable of defining a new class from a byte code. Once a class loader defines a class, it handles all classes used within that class. Aglets has a dedicated subclass of ClassLoader—AgletClassLoader. Each aglet object is associated with exactly one class loader, and it manages all classes required by that aglet. The same class loader may host other aglet objects. Suppose you have an aglet, MyAglet.

```
class MyAglet extends Aglets {
    MyDialog dialog = null;
    public void onCreation() {
        dialog = new MyDialog();
    }
}
```

Both the `MyAglet` class and the `MyDialog` class are managed by the same `Aglet-ClassLoader` object, and both of them are associated with the same code base, say `atp://some.server.com/public`.

It may happen that there are multiple sources of byte code for a given class. In that case, you may get unpredictable results from an aglet when a "wrong" class is being loaded and used. To avoid unnecessary confusion, it would probably be worth understanding which class definition is chosen by the class loader.

The `AgletClassLoader` maintains a cache table for classes formerly defined by the class loader, and it first looks up a class in that cache table. If it does not find it there, it asks the system class loader to load it from CLASSPATH. If this is also unsuccessful, it looks for the cached byte code in the `CacheManager`; if that also fails, it attempts to define the new class by loading byte code from the code base. Once the new class is defined, it is cached in the cache table and can be reused later by other aglets.

Let us take an example. If the class loader of `MyAglet` also loads the `MyAglet2` class, the cached class is used to resolve the `MyDialog` class. Because both the `java.lang.String` class and the `LocalClass` class are supposed to be available on the CLASSPATH, they will be loaded by the system class loader and then become system classes.

```
class MyAglet2 extends Aglets {
    // MyDialog class found in class cache.
    MyDialog dialog = null;
    // String class is system class, i.e., CLASSPATH.
    String str = "Hello";
    // LocalClass class is found in the CLASSPATH.
    LocalClass data = new LocalClass();
    public void onCreation(Object init) {
        dialog = new MyDialog();
    }
}
```

9.4.2   Class Transfer

As we mentioned, there are two possible ways of bringing byte code to the server. One way is to download and define a class on demand as the aglet moves, and the other approach is to transfer byte code along with the aglet as it moves. There are also some variants of these schemes, such as loading classes one by one or loading a set of classes at a time.

If you want to make robust aglets, an essential issue is to understand which classes are transferred and which ones are resident. You may not be able to execute your aglet at a remote site without having a thorough understanding of this issue. The Aglets framework classifies Java classes into four categories, according to where they come from, and manages them in different ways:

- *Archived classes*—classes that are archived in the JAR file.

- *Code base classes*—classes that are loaded from the aglet's code base.
- *System classes*—classes that are loaded from CLASSPATH and thus do not have a code base.
- *Others*—An aglet might refer to other classes that are loaded from other code bases by other aglets. This happens when an aglet receives a message that includes as an argument an object whose class was loaded from the sender's code base.

It is simple if the class is archived in the JAR file specified as the aglet's code base. All byte code in the archive is automatically transferred when the aglet moves and is maintained by the CacheManager. Therefore, if the MyAglet and MyDialog classes are archived in a JAR file, they are both transferred along with the aglet. Note that only one thing is guaranteed: that the byte code is transferred to its destination. The class actually defined and used by the aglet when it resumes execution at the destination is chosen according to the rule sketched above. For example, if the destination has the MyDialog class as a local system class in the CLASSPATH, then that local class will be used instead of the transferred one.

If no archive is being used, only classes loaded from within the code base are transferred along with the aglet. This means that all classes located in the aglet's code base can be transferred. However, system classes (located in the CLASSPATH) will never be transferred. In the MyAglet2 example, the byte code of LocalClass is not transferred, whereas the byte code of MyDialog is transferred.

The set of classes to be transferred is determined at runtime in the serialization process. That is, nonsystem classes of every object that is visited during the serialization are collected and transferred. Note that the class of a reference with a null value will not be transferred. What happens if such a null reference exists and the class is used after the aglet has been dispatched to a remote host? Let us take a look at the following example:

```
class MyAglet extends Aglet {
    MyDialog dialog = null;
    public void onCreation(Object init) {
        addMobilityListener(
          new MobilityAdapter() {
             public void onArrival(MobilityEvent ev) {
                // Create MyDialog object after arriving at the
                     destination.
                dialog = new MyDialog();
             }
          }
        );
        try {
        dispatch(destination);
        } catch (Exception ex) {
           ...
        }
    }
}
```

Because the `dialog` reference is `null`, the `MyDialog` class will not be transferred along with the dispatched aglet. Instead, the aglet will be sent without the `MyDialog` class and will then search for the `MyDialog` class on arrival. By following the class-loading rule explained earlier, the aglet may load the `MyDialog` class definition from the aglet's code base or it may use a locally cached class.

If you want to make sure that a certain class is actually transferred, you can either use a JAR archive or include a reference to the class's class instance.

```
class MyAglet extends Aglet {
    MyDialog dialog = null;
    // Refers to the class' class instance.
    Class class_used_later = MyDialog.class;
}
```

The Aglets framework will now transfer the `MyDialog` class along with the aglet.

Finally, if an aglet attempts to transfer an object whose class loader is different from the aglet's class loader, it fails with a `SecurityException`. This is because the Aglets framework, for security reasons, does not allow an aglet either to load a class from two different code bases or to take the byte code out of other aglets.

9.4.3   Class Resumption and Evolution

When an aglet arrives at a destination, the byte code in the network stream is retrieved and cached by `CacheManager`. The incoming byte code is then used by an `AgletClassLoader` to define the classes needed to reconstruct the aglet.

Because the Java language system does not allow you to define two classes with the same name in the same `ClassLoader`, the old class already stored in the cache may be used even if the updated class has been sent. This could cause a problem when objects are being deserialized, because the serialized data of the new class may be incompatible with those of the old version of that class, or, even worse, the classes could behave differently.

Let us take an example. `MyAglet` is a buggy aglet. It creates an instance of `MyDialog`, but it never explicitly shows the dialog.

```
// Version 1.
class MyAglet extends Aglet {
    MyDialog dialog = new MyDialog();
}
```

In the second version of `MyAglet`, we fix the problem by letting the `onCreation` method invoke `show()` on `MyDialog`.

```
// Version 2.
class MyAglet extends Aglet {
    MyDialog dialog = new MyDialog();
    public void onCreation(Object init) {
        dialog.show();  // Previously forgot to show the dialog...
    }
}
```

But even with that fix, you may still within the same session get the same result (the MyDialog does not open), because the first version of the MyAglet class most likely has been cached. Therefore, we must force a class definition to be updated as it evolves, while reducing the cost of transmitting and defining new classes. Aglets solves this problem by allocating different class loaders for different sets of classes. In the following discussion, we describe how a class loader is chosen.

To avoid the version conflict problem, the Aglets framework sends information about the names and versions of classes along with the classes' byte code. The AgletClassLoader stores similar information about defined classes. The version information is computed at runtime or is taken from the MANIFEST of the JAR archive. With this information, the receiver can determine which classes are used within the aglet even before receiving all the classes' byte code. As a result, the receiver can look up the appropriate ClassLoader that matches the given information in the cache. Note that only classes sent along with the aglet are version-checked by the class loader.

At the time of writing, the Aglets framework does not support automatic version detection when an aglet is created from a code base without using a JAR archive. We recommend you to use JAR archives to ensure proper version management of aglet classes.

Although we have so far focused on mechanisms for dispatching, the same schema is used for deactivation, activation, and cloning. The classes stored on persistent media are gathered by the rules described in the previous sections. Similarly, the ClassLoader used to activate aglets operates under the same conditions as those described earlier. Cloning an aglet results in the use of exactly the same ClassLoader as for the original aglet, and consequently the clone will consist of the same set of classes.

9.4.4 Other Considerations of Class Mobility

Currently, the Aglets framework does not attempt to optimize the transfer of byte code. The transport protocol does not perform checks to find out whether it needs to transfer a given class's byte code to a given destination. A "transfer only when needed" scheme has several drawbacks:

- It is not always faster than the current scheme.
- The source of classes for an aglet may be unavailable at the time it arrives owing to a fire wall or node failure.
- It might be possible to keep byte code in the cache at the sender node, but this raises the issue of when the byte code should be uploaded.

Aglets supports remote message passing, and aglet objects can communicate through messages remotely as well as locally. Argument objects and return values passed between messaging aglets can be of any Java class that implements `java.io.Serializable` or of any primitive Java type (`int`, `long`, and so on). Sending a remote message is different from dispatching an aglet in the sense that *a remote message does not cause any transfer of byte code*. Instead, the classes of objects passed along with a message must be available at both sites, either as system classes or as classes at the aglet's code base. If you want to send a message with a transfer of byte code, embed that message in an aglet.

9.5   Communication Layer

The Aglets runtime layer does not transfer aglets directly over the network. Instead, it uses the communication layer. The strength of this architecture is that it makes the runtime layer independent of the transport mechanism. The communication layer defines and implements a set of generic methods that support interagent messaging and transportation of an agent's state and associated byte code in a manner that is independent of the agent system.

9.5.1   Communication API

The communication API used by the Aglets runtime environment is derived from the OMG standard MASIF (Mobile Agent System Interoperability Facility), which allows various agent systems to interoperate. This API abstracts the communication layer by defining interfaces and by providing common representations of data. Although it is *not* a true CORBA interface, it is easy to implement a wrapper that actually uses MASIF objects.

We chose this approach because relying on a specific transport protocol or specific transport mechanisms has at least two disadvantages. First, requiring a mobile agent to use a specific protocol would be technically inappropriate unless that protocol were pervasive, because one of the benefits of mobile agents is their ability to hide the existence of network communication. Second, some Java environments, such as PersonalJava, support neither RMI nor CORBA in their core APIs. Therefore, it would be more desirable if the runtime environment could choose the communication mechanisms in accordance with its system requirements.

MASIF is a proposed standard for a CORBA environment that is intended to achieve interoperability between different agent systems but not for agents or other applications. It is normally used and implemented by agent system implementers. The focus of MASIF is on standardization of the following:

- Conceptual component definitions and their representations, such as the names of agents, places, and agent systems
- Information about agents and agent systems

- Location syntax
- Aglet creation and transfer
- Agent management
- Agent tracking

Two CORBA objects are defined in MASIF: `MAFAgentSystem` and `MAFFinder`. The `MAFAgentSystem` object defines methods for agent creation, transfer, and management.

Here is the IDL for `MAFAgentSystem`:

```
interface MAFAgentSystem {
    // Agent creation and transfer
    Name create_agent(in Name agent_name, ...) raises (..);
    void receive_agent(in Name agent_name,
                       in AgentProfile agent_profile,
                       in octet_string agent, ...) raises (..);
    // Agent management
    void get_agent_status(in Name agent_name) raises (..);
    void list_all_agents(in Name agent_name) raises (..);
    void suspend_agent(in Name agent_name) raises (..);
    void resume_agent(in Name agent_name) raises (..);
    void terminate_agent(in Name agent_name) raises (..);
    // etc...
}
```

To send an agent, the sender first locates the remote agent system object by means of normal CORBA services and by issuing the call `receive_agent()` on that remote agent system object with arguments that contain the agent's code and state.

`MAFFinder` is an object that provides a naming service for locating roaming agents. Its interface and functions are similar to those of the aglet in the `Aglet-Finder` example.

9.5.2 Agent Transfer Protocol

Agent Transfer Protocol is a simple application-level protocol modeled on HTTP. ATP is designed to transmit an agent independently of the agent system. An ATP request consists of a request line, header fields, and content. The request line specifies the method of the request, and the header fields contain the parameters of the request. ATP defines the following four standard request methods.

- *Dispatch* requests a destination agent system to reconstruct an agent from the content of a request and to start executing the agent. If the request is successful, the sender must terminate the agent and release any resources consumed by it.

- *Retract* requests that a destination agent system send the specified agent back to the sender. The receiver is responsible for reconstructing and resum-

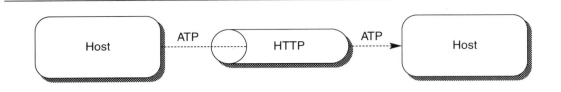

FIGURE 9-3   HTTP Tunneling of ATP

ing the agent. If the agent is successfully transferred, the receiver must terminate the agent and release any resources consumed by it.

- *Fetch* is similar to the GET method in HTTP; it requests that a receiver retrieve and send any identified information.

- *Message* is used to pass a message to the agent identified by an agent ID and to return a reply value. Although the protocol adopts a request/reply form, it does not lay down any rules for communication between agents.

Normally, an ATP server will attempt to make a direct connection to hosts in the network. However, most networks are protected by a fire wall that prevents users from opening direct socket connections to external nodes. Consequently, an aglet cannot be directly dispatched or retracted through a fire wall. To overcome this problem, ATP also supports a technique called *HTTP tunneling* (see Figure 9-3). This technique enables an ATP request to be sent outside the fire wall as an HTTP POST request; the response is retrieved as an HTTP response. In addition, the ATP server can be configured to accept HTTP-wrapped ATP requests with the content type application/x-atp. If an ATP server receives an HTTP-wrapped ATP request, it will reply with an HTTP response in the same way.

Because the fire wall allows only one-way connections to the outside, an aglet dispatched outside the fire wall cannot fetch a class inside the fire wall. Make sure that all necessary classes are stored in the stream and are transferred to the destination by making references to those classes inside the object, or put them together in the jar archive. Furthermore, it is impossible for an aglet to dispatch itself back through the fire wall. To get an aglet back inside a fire wall, you need to use retraction to pull the aglet from a remote site.

9.6   Summary

In this chapter we described some of the inner workings of the Aglets framework. It consists of three layers. On the top is the application layer, which contains the user-defined aglets. These aglets interface with the Aglet API and its implementation, the Aglets runtime layer. At the bottom is the Communication API and its implementation. To help you to improve the design of your aglets, we described a number of important elements of these layers. We looked at the aglet object structure, including the message manager and the resource manager. We also discussed aglet initialization as well as aglet serialization and object mobility and explained how class loading and class transfer work in the Aglets framework. We described class resumption and evolution in the Aglets framework. In addition, we showed you the Communication API in some detail and discussed the use of the Agent Transfer Protocol.

We also described aglet initialization as well as aglet serialization and object mobility, and explained how class loading and class transfer work in the aglet framework. In addition, we discussed the issue of class resumption and evolution, and how to cope with them.

Chapter 10 covers a key topic raised by the use of mobile agents: security.

Chapter 10
Aglet Security

With the Internet, and in particular the Web, becoming increasingly popular and with electronic commerce starting to take off, security seems more important than ever. With proper security in place, people will no longer hesitate to purchase goods and exchange confidential information via the Internet. Indeed, security is one of the key factors in the breakthrough of mobile agent technology. Like any other downloadable and executable code, mobile agents are a potential threat to a system. But they are also exposed to threats by their hosting system, a situation not currently dealt with in traditional security systems. In the absence of a simple but comprehensive agent security mechanism, users will not readily use agents or accept any mobile agents visiting their computers, and we will not see widespread deployment of mobile agents. In this chapter you will learn about network security technologies in general and mobile agent security in particular.

We will first show you what can go wrong when mobile agents are released in a network. This discussion is followed by a taxonomy of security attacks related to mobile agents. We then explain security services that protect agents and servers against these attacks, followed by a discussion of the inherent limitations of agent security. The remainder of the chapter outlines a security model for aglets.

10.1 What Can Go Wrong?

Suppose you dispatch a ticket reservation agent to a box office. What are the risks? First, your agent might be tampered with. As a result, it might report invalid results; for example, it might tell you that a reservation has been made when in reality it has not. A malicious host might also extract (steal) and use confidential information from your agent. Even more hideous, someone might tamper with your agent so that it will harm the remote host that it is visiting. In that case, you might be considered liable and barred from using the service in the future. How could you prove that you are innocent?

These are just a few examples of what can go wrong for mobile agents. We can divide security threats from mobile agents into the following categories.

- *Agent protection*

  Remote host threatens agent. An agent is on a trip and visits an untrusted server that may attempt to extract private information from or tamper with the agent. Possible attack types include tampering, illegal execution, and illegal access.

  Agent threatens another agent. An agent interacts with one of your agents in an attempt to extract private information from it and to interrupt its execution. A possible attack type is illegal access.

  Unauthorized third parties threaten agent. A malicious entity may alter messages exchanged between hosts or tap the communication between them and reveal the content of your agent. Possible attack types include altering and eavesdropping.

- *Host protection*

  Incoming agent threatens host. An incoming agent visiting a server attempts to access and corrupt the host's private files or interrupts the server. Possible attacks include illegal access, masquerade, Trojan horse, denial of service, and repudiation.

  Unauthorized third parties threaten host. A malicious entity may send a large number of "spam" agents to a server to take it out of service. Possible attacks include denial of service and replay.

- *Network protection*

  Incoming agent threatens the network. An agent starts multiplying and traveling extensively in an attempt to flood the network with agents. Possible attack is denial of service.

Although such threats involve relatively new security issues raised by mobile agent technology, using existing security technology can solve most of them. In the next section, we discuss each type of attack in detail.

10.2   Taxonomy of Attacks

Now we'll introduce some possible security attacks related to mobile agents. In general, we can divide attacks on agents and their hosts into two categories:

passive attacks that do not modify the agents and other information, and *active attacks* that actually do something to the agents. In an active attack you may detect that something has happened to your agent, whereas that is not the case for a passive attack.

10.2.1 Passive Attacks

Passive attacks are typically attempted against communicating agent systems and agents being transferred in a network. Because no changes are made to the agents, such attacks are normally difficult to detect. To protect themselves, agent users should employ cryptography (described later in this chapter). Let us look at two kinds of passive attack.

Eavesdropping This type of attack normally uses a program called a communication monitor. A monitor keeps watching information exchanged between agent systems, thereby capturing agents and messages that may contain useful information (see Figure 10-1). More generally, we can say that information is revealed through monitoring of communications.

Traffic Analysis You may think that it is easy to prevent eavesdropping by using encrypting agents. Although this technique might be enough in most cases, passive attacks can still be effective. *Traffic analysis*, which is an intelligent variant of eavesdropping, allows the attacker to analyze the patterns of agents exchanged between agent systems (for things such as changes in the amount of traffic or changes in the frequency of incoming and outgoing agents), perhaps enabling him or her to make certain assumptions based on these patterns. This kind of attack is effective even if the content is encrypted.

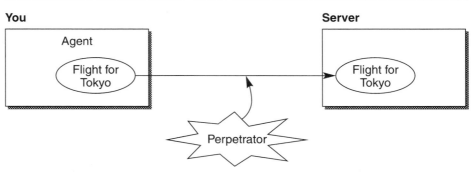

FIGURE 10-1 Eavesdropping

10.2.2   Active Attacks

Active attacks involve a wide variety of security threats, ranging from simple modification of the agents' data to injection of malicious agents into unknowing servers. Let's look at some types of active attacks.

Illegal Access   An agent accesses information it is not allowed to access. This may happen if the agent masquerades as a trusted user or is executed in an unsafe execution environment. For example, if an agent is written in the C programming language, it can use pointer arithmetic to access arbitrary memory locations. Not only can the agent retrieve private data from the host and other agents on that host, but it can also tamper with the data.

Masquerade   An entity pretends to be a different entity (see Figure 10-2). In a typical example, an agent enters a server by seemingly representing a trusted person or organization. If it succeeds in deceiving the host, it may be able to use a service for free or steal confidential information reserved for the trusted entity.

Trojan Horse   A Trojan horse is an agent that is executed by a legitimate user but does something different from what the user expects or approves (see Figure 10-3). A perpetrator can simply create and perhaps launch an innocent-looking agent that in reality is harmful to its users.

Alteration   An agent or message between two agent systems is deleted or changed while in transit (see Figure 10-4). In particular, any host visited on the agent's itinerary may strip data added by previous hosts. Any information that is modified in an unexpected way may turn a sound agent into a malicious one or may simply return false results.

Replay   A captured copy of a previously sent legitimate agent is retransmitted for illegitimate purposes (see Figure 10-5). In this way, the perpetrator may be

FIGURE 10-2   Masquerade

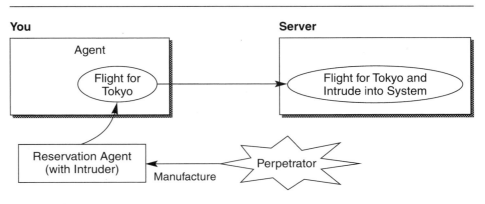

FIGURE 10-3 Trojan Horse

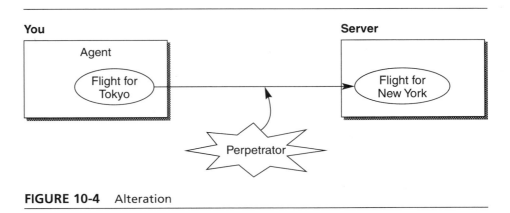

FIGURE 10-4 Alteration

able to obtain identical results or may fatally disturb the service. Even if the agent is encrypted, such an attack is still possible, because the attacker need not change the agent's content.

Resource Exhaustion A resource is deliberately used so heavily that service to other users is disrupted. This is also known as a *denial of service* (DOS) attack. The resource in question can be network bandwidth as well as server memory or a CPU. For example, if a malicious agent keeps allocating memory, other agents or perhaps the server itself may be rendered unable to operate properly. Another example is the use of agents that keep cloning. Soon the server or the network will be "filled" with agents.

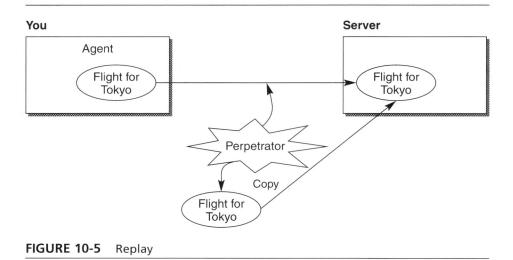

FIGURE 10-5   Replay

Repudiation   A party to a communication exchange later denies that the exchange took place. For example, if your agent purchases something via an agent server, the server may later deny the deal.

10.3   Security Services

Security services are important if you wish to protect your agents and servers against attacks. The following is a list of commonly available services for securing agent systems.

- *Authentication.* Before accepting an incoming agent, you want to know who its sender is. In this case, you need authenticate the agent. This process includes verifying the entity that developed (programmed) the agent and the entity that instantiated it and dispatched it to you. Before sending an agent, you may want to verify that the destination server is indeed the server that it says it is. Here is more detail:

  Authentication of user.   The user needs to authenticate himself or herself to a given server. Public-key encryption or a password can be used for this purpose.

  Authentication of host.   Before a server starts to communicate with another server or client, it needs to know with whom it is communicating. This is important, because you cannot ensure integrity and confidentiality without knowing whom you are receiving agents from or sending agents to.

Authentication of code. Before executing an incoming agent, the server needs to know who is responsible for the agent's implementation. Digital signatures are typically used for this purpose.

Authentication of agent. Before executing an incoming agent, the server needs to know who is responsible for this agent (owner). As we will describe later, this is a problem without a clear solution.

- *Integrity.* To rely on an agent, you need to make sure that no one has tampered with its state and code. Checking the integrity of the agent is the technique we use to verify that no illegitimate alterations have been made to the state and code of an agent.

- *Confidentiality.* An agent may carry confidential (private) information that should be readable only by particular servers or agents. Such information should be kept secret from other servers and agents. An agent may request a server to transport itself in a secret way to cope with an eavesdropping threat.

- *Authorization.* An incoming agent should be given a right to access information according to its principals. Authorization, or access control, is the way to specify and enforce an agent's capability to access information or to use services provided by a server.

- *Nonrepudiation.* An agent or server cannot deny that a given communication exchange has taken place.

- *Auditing.* An auditing service records security-related activities of an agent for later inspection.

10.4 What Is Possible and What Is Not: When You Cannot Protect Your Agents

It is essential to be aware that there are certain inherent limits to agent security. Let us take a closer look at this statement from two views: agent protection and host protection.

The protection of your agents relies heavily on the server that they visit. The first threat that mobile agents encounter is when they are transferred over the wire of a network. There may be eavesdroppers that attempt to retrieve private information from the agents. Untrusted third parties may also tamper with the content of your agents, leading to unwanted behavior of the agents. Fortunately, this kind of attack is easy to handle and can be solved by using classic techniques. An ordinary secure connection, such as Secure Sockets Layer (SSL)—which can encrypt the data and check their integrity—can be used to effectively avoid this kind of attack.

The next threat is the remote server that the agents visit. When you send an agent to a remote server, you expect that the server will treat your agent properly

Cryptography and Digital Signing

Let us add a few words about some of the fundamental technologies behind many security services, namely, *cryptography* and *digital signing*. You can safely skip this section if you already know the basics of cryptography.

With cryptography and digital signing, you can ensure confidentiality, authentication, and integrity. Let us briefly go over some of the techniques used in cryptography and digital signing.

Secret-key encryption, also called *conventional encryption*, uses one key that is shared by the sender and receiver sides. The sender encrypts the agent using the shared key, and the receiver decrypts the encrypted agent using the same key. The advantage of secret-key encryption is its speed. The disadvantage is that it requires a secure and scalable key management distribution system to effectively distribute secret keys to users. Therefore, this technique is often used in conjunction with public-key encryption such as in Secure Sockets Layer (SSL).

Whereas secret-key encryption uses one shared key to encrypt and decrypt data, *public-key cryptography* uses two different keys to encrypt and decrypt data. One key, called the *private key*, should be kept secret, whereas the other key, called the *public key*, can be distributed to the public. Although each of these keys can be used for both encryption and decryption, the data encrypted with one key can be decrypted only with the other key. To send an agent in a confidential way, the sender encrypts the agent with the receiver's public key and sends it. The receiver, on the other hand, decrypts the agent by using its private key. Because only the receiver knows its private key and because the encrypted message cannot be decrypted with any key except the private key, the sender and the receiver can exchange messages securely.

The advantage of public-key encryption is that the receiver of the encrypted agent need not have a secret key, so the key distribution problem is eliminated.

and will serve any valid requests the agent may make. Suppose your agent requests access to a database. On the basis of the information the agent retrieves, it may request that the server send it to another competing server in search of, say, a better bargain. As an agent owner you need to consider the following issues.

10.4.1   Agent Execution

Remember that the agent is totally in the hands of the remote server. Although we often claim that agents are autonomous, they are not independent processors that can execute their own programs. The server is entirely responsible for the execution of the agent, and it is left to the server whether the agent is executed properly. The server may also give the agent wrong information to mislead it.

Even the agent's travel plan is not safe. A server may not allow your agent to travel to a competing server, instead sending it to a conspiring server. Needless to

The disadvantage of public-key encryption is its slow speed. It is normally 100 to 1,000 times slower than secret-key encryption. Because of this disadvantage, you will often find that this shortcut is used: a sender uses a randomly generated secret key to encrypt an entire agent and then encrypts the secret key by using the public key of the destination, sending both the encrypted agent and the key.

With a *digital signature* it is possible to verify the originator of an agent signed by the originator or to check the integrity of an agent signed by the sender. Because public-key encryption works "both ways," this technique can also be used to sign data. A signer encrypts the agent with the signer's private key. If a receiver can decrypt the encrypted agent by using the signer's public key, it proves that the signature is valid.

Obviously, we need a secure way of ensuring that distributed public keys really represent the organizations they purport to represent. A solution to this problem is to use a trusted third party called a *certification authority* (CA). The CA issues a certificate that contains the name of the party and the associated public key. The CA then *signs* this certificate with its private key. Because only the CA can generate the signed certificate, it guarantees the mapping of the name of an organization and its public key provided that you trust the CA.

A secure *one-way hash algorithm* is a transformation algorithm that transforms a given data set into a relatively short hash value. A key property of a secure one-way hash algorithm is that there is no simple way of finding the original value from a given hash value. From an original value, the secure hash value can generate a fixed and short value that allows us to assume the correspondence between the original and the hash value. In other words, if two hash values are given and they are the same, we can infer that the two original data sets are identical. This technique is often used to condense data while keeping its uniqueness. For example, it is less costly to digitally sign a hash value than to sign the entire content.

say, therefore, critical decision making by an agent should take place only on trusted hosts.

10.4.2   Information That Is Secret to Servers

Because all information necessary for processing an agent must be readable to the server, the server has the potential to steal, tamper with, or leak any of the agent's information. For example, what if the agent carries an access key for a specific server and that key must be kept secret from other servers that the agent may visit? One possible solution is to encrypt the access key with the server's public key. Then that server would be the only server that could decrypt and use the key.

What if the agent is given secret data at a given server? One way to protect such data would be to directly send them back to the owner of the agent. The agent can also choose to encrypt the received data with the owner's public key.

However, this must be done with the help of the server. Other servers then have no way to read the data.

Note that an agent cannot generate secret information without the help of the interpreter (the server) and thus cannot keep anything created at the server secret from it. This implies that agents cannot keep communications with other agents secret from the server.

10.4.3   Information Secret from Other Agents

Even if you expect your agent to be protected from other agents, the server may allow other agents to retrieve information from your agent. Other agents may also, if allowed by the server, tamper with a given agent. The bottom line is that if you do not trust a server, you cannot expect much security for your agents that visit it. If you want secure execution, you should send agents only to servers you trust.

10.5   When You Cannot Trust Incoming Agents

Suppose you are the administrator of a merchant server that allows visiting agents to access a product database. If someone sends an agent to the server and you find that the agent presents correct ownership, it is not expected to harm your server, and it should perform its task in a predictable and reliable way. As the person responsible for a server, however, you need to consider the following issues.

10.5.1   Agent Masquerading as a Trusted User

Because the activities performed by a given agent should be controlled by the owner's authority, it is important that an agent present its true ownership. If an incoming agent masquerades as a trusted user, it can do whatever the trusted user can do. For example, in a subscription-based service, fees could be wrongly charged to a user's account. Therefore, agents need to be properly authenticated. However, carrying the user's password or private key is too unsafe and thus is not an acceptable solution. Signing the entire agent would not work, because its state varies over its lifetime.

If you want to know only who made the agent program, it is relatively simple. Digital signatures can effectively prove the identity of the manufacturer or programmer. However, this technique cannot be applied to the state of an agent because the state will vary over the agent's lifetime. There is no way to verify the current state, because it is the result of program execution, so it is hard to authenticate the agent itself.

There are several ways to improve the process of verifying an agent's authenticity. For example, if a portion of the state remains static over its life cycle, it can be signed by the owner. In addition, assertions can be used to verify that the dynamic state of an agent is within the valid range.

10.5.2   Agent Is Tampered With

This means not only tampering with an agent's code but also altering the agent's state. Suppose that you launch an agent that visits a remote site to perform a database query. If the destination site simply exchanges the agent's destination server and home server information and sends it back to the server it came from, the agent may retrieve information from your database before it "returns" to the destination server. Again, if you want to verify the program, that's simple. But if you want to verify the state in a general way, it's difficult. One typical solution is the organizational approach. Following this approach, we create a group of servers that mutually trust one another. Any server in the group must be authenticated as the member of that group in order to communicate and send an agent to another member of the group.

10.5.3   Agent Exceeds Its Authority and Harms the Server

Even if the agent represents the correct identity, there is still the danger of being attacked. The program may have been tampered with so that it illegally accesses private information, or a malfunctioning agent may cause harm to the server.

As we mentioned, you can easily use digital signatures to verify that no attempt has been made to tamper with the agent. This verification, however, guarantees nothing about the agent's behavior and does not protect the agent system from illegal access. Thus, the agent system must equipped with the following properties:

- *Language safety.* Any facility that enables illegal access to the system memory or private information must be strictly prohibited.

- *Authorization enforcement.* All agents must be strictly controlled under the security policy defined by the authority. There should be no way to get around this policy.

10.6   Security Model

Now let's look at a security model that provides an overall framework for aglet security. The model supports the definition of security policies and describes how and where a secure aglet system enforces these policies. The described model is based on Aglets SDK 1.1 Beta 1 and subject to change.

We will start by describing the principals of the model, that is, the entities whose identity can be authenticated. We will then cover the authentication process before finishing with a description of the access control mechanism (authorization), which defines a policy specifying what an aglet can and cannot do.

10.6.1   Principals

Who are the principals within an aglet system? These principals are authenticated identities that are used to enforce the policies defined by authorities and to identify the developer of the program or the host it is communicating with. Our model identifies several fundamental principals: the aglet, the aglet owner, the aglet manufacturer, the context, the domain, and the domain authority.

Aglet   Because of the autonomous behavior of aglets, it is reasonable to assume that they can define their own security policy and request all servers to honor it. An aglet may, for example, define a policy that allows only aglets owned by the same user to access it. There are three roles for aglet principals:

- *Aglet.* An aglet object is actually the thread responsible for executing the aglet.

- *Aglet manufacturer.* The aglet manufacturer represents the person or organization that implemented the aglet program. The behavior of aglets should also be controlled under the permissions given to that aglet program.

- *Aglet owner.* The aglet owner represents the person or organization that instantiated and launched the aglet. Because an owner is responsible for its aglet, this principal is used for authorization or accounting of the aglet.

Context and Server   Contexts and servers are responsible for keeping the underlying operating system safe by protecting it from malicious aglets. A server defines a minimal security policy to protect local resources. Each context, on the other hand, is responsible for hosting visiting aglets, and it provides access to appropriate local resources. Therefore, each context on a single server may define a different security policy according to its particular responsibility. For example, a context that serves a database may allow aglets to access the database, whereas other contexts on the same server may not allow such access. The possible items that a server and a context may define include an aglet's access to local resources such as file system, windows, and network connections; runtime resources, such as memory and CPU time, that an aglet can consume; the maximum number of aglets that can visit at one time; and limitations on the activities of aglets, such as the maximum number of instances or clones that an aglet can create and the lifetime of an aglet. There are three roles for context and server principals:

- *Context.* A context is a place that hosts aglets. Actually, it is an operating system process executing on the server that hosts the context.

- *Context manufacturer.* This is the manufacturer of a context server. As with aglets, it is in a manufacturer's interest that no one be able to claim damage caused by a malfunctioning context and server.

- *Context owner.* The context represents the context owner. This principal is used for authenticating hosts in the role of sender and receiver of aglets.

Network Domain The domain represents the group of servers. The principal of the domain authority is used to authenticate whether a server is a member of its domain. For example, a server can verify whether a communicating server belongs to the same domain by making sure that the destination has the certificate issued by the domain authority.

A network domain authority is responsible for keeping its network secure so that all incoming aglets can complete their tasks safely. For example, because bandwidth is the key resource used by an aglet to successfully transport itself to the next destination, bandwidth must be protected properly. Resources that may need to be protected include the number of hops that an aglet can perform, the number of clones that an aglet can spawn, and the lifetime of an aglet within a domain. Further protection may be provided according to the domain. For example, a domain may define the maximum number of queries that an aglet can issue to a database in that domain.

10.6.2 Permissions

Permissions define the capabilities of executing aglets by setting access restrictions and limits on resource consumption. Permission is a resource, such as a local file, together with appropriate actions such as reading or writing a file, listening to a network port, or creating a desktop window. An abstract syntax for permissions in Aglets is based on JDK 1.2 policy file definition, *[permission name action]*. Please refer to the latest documentation of JDK 1.2 and Aglets SDK for more details.

Several permissions are available for aglets:

- *File permission.* Access to the local file system is also subject to control. The aglet can be granted access to a specific file or an entire directory.

```
FilePermission "/tmp/*" "read,write"
FilePermission "C:\public\*" "read"
```

- *Network permissions.* As with file permission, access to the network is also subject to control. The aglet can be granted access to a specific host or to listen on a specific port.

```
SocketPermissions "trl.ibm.com:100-100" "connect"
SocketPermissions "trl.ibm.com:100-300" "listen,connect,accept"
```

- *Window system.* An aglet can be granted permission to open a window.

  ```
  AWTPermission "topLevelWindow"
  ```

- *Context permission.* An aglet can be granted permission to use services provided by the context. This includes access to methods for creating, cloning, dispatching, retracting, deactivating, and activating aglets.

  ```
  ContextPermission "examples.HelloAglet" "create"
  ContextPermission "context" "start,remove"
  ```

- *Aglet permission.* The methods provided by an individual aglet are subject to control. An aglet can be allowed to invoke methods in another aglet owned by a principal given by a name.

  ```
  AgletPermission "Oshima" "dispose"
  AgletPermission "*" "dispatch"
  ```

10.6.3   Protections

Although an aglet may be granted access to a resource or other aglets, it may also want to protect itself from access by other entities. For example, it is reasonable for you to request that an aglet be disposed of only by you, whereas other methods may be publicly accessible. Protections define the level of protection by setting access restrictions.

```
AgletProtection "Oshima" "dispose"
AgletProtection "*" "dispatch"
```

Note that protections require that the host honor them. This also means that the host administrator, for example, may override a protection policy in order to dispose of aglets.

10.6.4   Policy and Authority

All the principals we've introduced—aglet, aglet manufacturer, aglet owner, context, context manufacturer, context owner, network domain owner, and the permissions and protections—may define *security policies*. A security policy is formulated as a set of rules denoted by principals and privileges. The policy file definition in Aglets is based on JDK 1.2.

It is a policy authority that defines these policies. A policy authority is the person or organization responsible for resources consumed by other entities. For example, an aglet owner is responsible for the aglet itself, whereas the context owner authority is responsible for keeping the server and machine safe. In our model there are three authorities:

- *Aglet owner.* Because of the autonomous behavior of aglets, it is reasonable to assume that they can define their own security policy. The main objective of the aglet owner is to protect the aglet from attacks. The aglet owner may define security policies for his or her aglets. When aglets are visiting a context they may *request* the context to enforce the specific policy. It is, however, up to the context and context owner whether to grant this policy enforcement. The context owner is above the aglet owner in the security hierarchy and need not wholly agree with the aglet owner's security policy.

```
grant codebase "http://some.host.com", ownedby "Oshima" {
        protection.com.ibm.aglet.security.AgletProtection
                    "Oshima" "dispose";
    }
```

- *Context owner.* A context authority is responsible for keeping the server and the underlying system safe from malicious aglets. The context owner's security policy defines the actions an aglet can take in a given context.

```
grant codebase "http://some.host.com",
        signedBy "IBM",
        ownedBy "Oshima" {
            permission java.io.FilePermission
            "/tmp/file.dat" "read"; permission java.awt.AWTPermission
            "topLevelWindow"; permission java.net.SocketPermission
            "www.trl.ibm.co.jp:80" "connect";
    }
```

- *Network domain owner.* A network domain authority is responsible for keeping its network secure so that the servers within the domain can provide their services safely and all incoming aglets can complete their tasks. The domain authority defines the security policy for the domain. For example, it may put restrictions on the number of hops that an incoming aglet can make or on the lifetime of an aglet so that the aglet will be disposed of when its lifetime has expired.

10.7 Summary

In the first part of this chapter, we analyzed the risks associated with mobile agents. We divided the security threats into the following categories: remote host threatens agent, agent threatens another agent, unauthorized third parties threaten agent, incoming agent threatens host, unauthorized third parties threaten host, and incoming agent threatens the network. Based on this analysis we presented a taxonomy of attacks and a set of security services aimed at dealing with them. The chapter concluded with an overview of the aglet security model. This model supports the definition of security policies and describes how and where a secure aglet system enforces these policies.

Appendix

The Aglet API Documentation

A.1 `com.ibm.aglet` Package

A.1.1 Interface com.ibm.aglet.AgletContext

Interface **AgletContext** `public interface AgletContext`

The `AgletContext` interface is used by an aglet to get information about its environment and to send messages to the environment and other aglets currently active in that environment. It provides means for maintaining and managing running aglets in an environment where the host system is secured against malicious aglets.

A.1.1.1 Methods

`public abstract String` **getName()**

Gets the name of the context. Contexts running in the same server can be distinguished by their name.

`public abstract Enumeration` **getAgletProxies(int type)**

Gets the collection of aglet proxies in the context. Specify type as either `Aglet.ACTIVE` or `Aglet.INACTIVE`.

```
public abstract AgletProxy getAgletProxy(AgletID identity)
```
Gets a proxy for an aglet in the current context. The selected aglet is specified by its identity.

```
public abstract AgletProxy createAglet(URL codeBase, String
code, Object init) throws IOException, AgletException, ClassNot-
FoundException, InstantiationException
```
Creates an instance of the specified aglet class. The aglet's class code file can be located on the local file system as well as on a remote server. If the code base is null, the context will search for the code in the local system's aglet search path.

```
public abstract AgletProxy retractAglet(URL location, AgletID
identity) throws IOException, AgletException
```
Retracts the aglet specified by its location and identity.

```
public abstract ReplySet multicastMessage(Message msg)
```
Sends a multicast message to the subscribers in the context.

```
public abstract URL getHostingURL()
```
Returns the location of the daemon serving this context.

```
public abstract void showDocument(URL location)
```
Loads and displays a document from the specified location.

```
public abstract Object getProperty(String key)
```
Gets the context property indicated by the key.

```
public abstract Object getProperty(String key, Object default)
```
Gets the context property indicated by the key. Returns a default value if the property key cannot be found.

```
public abstract void setProperty(String key, Object value)
```
Sets the context property indicated by the key and value.

```
public abstract Image getImage(URL image)
```
Gets an image.

```
public abstract AudioClip getAudioClip(URL location)
```
Gets an audio clip.

```
public abstract ImageData getImageData(URL location)
```
Gets image data.

```
public abstract Image getImage(ImageData image)
```
Gets an image.

public abstract void **addContextListener(ContextListener listener)**

Adds the specified context listener to receive context events from this context.

public abstract void **removeContextListener(ContextListener listener)**

Removes the specified context listener.

public abstract void **start()**

Starts the context. Ignored if the context is already running.

public abstract void **clearCache(URL codebase)**

Clears the in-memory cache.

public abstract void **shutdown(Message msg)**

Shuts down the context with the specific message object. This message object is delivered to all aglets in the context before all aglets are killed. This is ignored if the context is already stopped.

public abstract void **shutdown()**

Shuts down the context. Is ignored if the context is already stopped.

A.1.2   Interface com.ibm.aglet.AgletProxy

Interface **AgletProxy** public interface AgletProxy

AgletProxy interface is a placeholder for aglets. The purpose of this interface is to provide a mechanism to control and limit direct access to aglets.

A.1.2.1 Methods

public abstract Aglet **getAglet()** throws InvalidAgletException

Gets the aglet that the proxy manages.

public abstract AgletID **getAgletID()** throws InvalidAgletException

Gets the aglet's identity.

public abstract String **getAgletClassName()** throws InvalidAglet-Exception

Gets the aglet's class name.

public abstract AgletInfo **getAgletInfo()** throws InvalidAglet-Exception

Gets the AgletInfo object of the aglet.

public abstract Object **clone()** throws CloneNotSupportedException

Clones the aglet and its proxy.

`public abstract` AgletProxy **dispatch(URL destination)** `throws IOException, AgletException`

Dispatches the aglet to the destination specified by the argument address.

`public abstract void` **dispose()** `throws InvalidAgletException`

Disposes of the aglet.

`public abstract void` **deactivate(long duration)** `throws IOException, InvalidAgletException`

Deactivates the aglet. The aglet will automatically be activated when the specified period has elapsed.

`public abstract void` **activate()** `throws IOException, AgletException`

Activates the aglet. This is a forced activation of a deactivated aglet.

`public abstract` Object **sendMessage(Message msg)** `throws Invalid-AgletException, NotHandledException, MessageException`

Sends a synchronous message to the aglet.

`public abstract` FutureReply **sendAsyncMessage(Message msg)** `throws InvalidAgletException`

Sends an asynchronous message to the aglet.

`public abstract` FutureReply **sendFutureMessage(Message msg)** `throws InvalidAgletException`

Sends a future message to the aglet.

`public abstract void` **sendOnewayMessage(Message msg)** `throws Invalid-AgletException`

Sends a one-way message to the aglet.

`public abstract void` **delegateMessage(Message msg)** `throws Invalid-AgletException`

Delegates a message to the aglet.

`public abstract boolean` **isActive()** `throws InvalidAgletException`

Checks whether the aglet is active.

`public abstract boolean` **isValid()**

Checks whether the aglet proxy is valid.

`public abstract boolean` **isRemote()**

Checks whether the aglet proxy is managing a remote aglet.

`public abstract boolean` **isState(int state)**

Checks whether the aglet is in a given state.

A.1.3   Interface com.ibm.aglet.MessageManager

Interface **MessageManager** public interface MessageManager

The MessageManager controls concurrency of incoming messages. Each kind of message has a priority and will be placed in the message queue in accordance with its priority.

A.1.3.1 Variables

public final static int **NOT_QUEUED**

A priority that indicates that a given kind of message should not be queued.

public final static int **ACTIVATE_AGLET**

A priority that indicates that a given kind of message can activate deactivated aglets.

public final static int **MIN_PRIORITY**

The minimal priority that the message can have.

public final static int **NORM_PRIORITY**

The default priority that is assigned to a message.

public final static int **MAX_PRIORITY**

The maximum priority that the message can have.

A.1.3.2   Methods

public abstract void **waitMessage()**

Waits until it is notified.

public abstract void **waitMessage(long duration)**

Waits until it is notified or the specified period has elapsed.

public abstract void **notifyMessage()**

Notifies a single waiting thread.

public abstract void **notifyAllMessages()**

Notifies all waiting threads.

public abstract void **exitMonitor()**

Exits the current monitor.

public abstract void **setPriority(String kind, int priority)**

Sets the priority of the specified kind of message.

public abstract void **destroy()**

Destroys the message manager. All queued and incoming messages will be rejected.

A.1.4   Class com.ibm.aglet.Aglet

public class **Aglet** implements Serializable

The Aglet class is the abstract base class for aglets. Use this class to create your own personalized aglets.

A.1.4.1 Variables

public final static short **MAJOR_VERSION**

The aglet's major version number.

public final static short **MINOR_VERSION**

The aglet's minor version number.

public final static int **ACTIVE**

Active state of aglet.

public final static int **INACTIVE**

Inactive state of aglet.

A.1.4.2   Methods

public final Object **clone()** throws CloneNotSupportedException

Clones the aglet and the proxy that holds the aglet. Notice that it is the cloned aglet proxy that is returned by this method.

public final void **dispatch(URL destination)** throws IOException, RequestRefusedException

Dispatches the aglet to the specified destination.

public final void **dispose()**

Destroys and removes the aglet from its current aglet context.

public final void **deactivate(long duration)** throws IOException

Deactivates the aglet. The aglet will temporarily be stopped. It will resume execution after the specified period has elapsed.

public final void **snapshot()** throws IOException

Saves a snapshot of this aglet's state.

public void **run()**

The entry point for the aglet's own thread of execution. This method is invoked upon a successful creation, dispatch, retraction, or activation of the aglet.

public void **onCreation(Object init)**

Initializes the new aglet. This method is called only once in the life cycle of an aglet. Override this method for custom initialization of the aglet.

public final void **addCloneListener(CloneListener listener)**

Adds the specified clone listener to receive clone events for this aglet.

public final void **addMobilityListener(MobilityListener listener)**

Adds the specified mobility listener to receive mobility events for this aglet.

public final void **addPersistencyListener(PersistencyListener listener)**

Adds the specified persistency listener to receive persistency events for this aglet.

public final void **removeCloneListener(CloneListener listener)**

Removes the specified clone listener.

public final void **removeMobilityListener(MobilityListener listener)**

Removes the specified mobility listener.

public final void **removePersistencyListener(PersistencyListener listener)**

Removes the specified persistency listener.

public void **onDisposing()**

Called when an attempt is made to dispose of the aglet. Subclasses may override this method to implement actions that should be taken in response to a request for disposal.

public boolean **handleMessage(Message message)**

Handles incoming messages.

public void **waitMessage()**

Waits until it is notified.

public void **waitMessage(long duration)**

Waits until it is notified or specified period has elapsed.

public void **notifyMessage()**

Notifies a single waiting thread.

public void **notifyAllMessages()**

Notifies all waiting threads.

public final AgletProxy **getProxy()**

Retrieves the proxy for the aglet.

public void **exitMonitor()**
Exits the current monitor.

public final AgletContext **getAgletContext()**
Gets the context in which the aglet is currently executing.

public final MessageManager **getMessageManager()**
Gets the message manager.

public final AgletID **getAgletID()**
Gets the aglet's identity.

public final URL **getCodeBase()**
Gets the aglet's code base.

public final AgletInfo **getAgletInfo()**
Gets the aglet's information object.

public final String **getText()**
Gets the aglet's message line.

public final void **setText(String text)**
Sets the aglet's message line.

public final void **subscribeMessage(String name)**
Subscribes to a named message.

public final boolean **unsubscribeMessage(String name)**
Unsubscribes from a named message.

public final void **unsubscribeAllMessages()**
Unsubscribes from all kinds of messages.

public final Image **getImage(URL location)** throws IOException
Gets an image.

public final Image **getImage(URL location, String name)** throws IOException
Gets an image.

public final AudioClip **getAudioData(URL location)** throws IOException
Gets audio data.

A.1.5 Class com.ibm.aglet.AgletID

public class **AgletID** implements Serializable

The AgletID class represents the unique identifier given to the aglet.

A.1.5.1 Methods

public boolean **equals(Object obj)**

Compares two aglet identifiers.

A.1.6 Class com.ibm.aglet.AgletInfo

public final class **AgletInfo** implements Externalizable

AgletInfo class defines an object that contains information about an aglet.

A.1.6.1 Methods

public AgletID **getAgletID()**

Gets the aglet's identity.

public String **getAgletClassName()**

Gets the aglet's class name.

public String **getOrigin()**

Gets the aglet's origin location.

public URL **getCodeBase()**

Gets the aglet's code base.

public String **getAddress()**

Gets the aglet's current location.

public long **getCreationTime()**

Gets the time when the aglet was created.

public short **getAPIMajorVersion()**

Gets the API's major version number.

public short **getAPIMinorVersion()**

Gets the API's minor version number.

A.1.7   Class `com.ibm.aglet.FutureReply`

`public class` **FutureReply**

The `FutureReply` class is an abstract class for future messages.

A.1.7.1 Methods

`public abstract Object` **getReply()** `throws MessageException, Not-HandledException`

Gets an `Object` reply.

`public int` **getIntReply()** `throws MessageException, NotHandled-Exception`

Gets the reply as a primitive integer.

`public double` **getDoubleReply()** `throws MessageException, Not-HandledException`

Gets the reply as a primitive double.

`public float` **getFloatReply()** `throws MessageException, Not-HandledException`

Gets the reply as a primitive float.

`public boolean` **getBooleanReply()** `throws MessageException, Not-HandledException`

Gets the reply as a primitive Boolean.

`public char` **getCharReply()** `throws MessageException, NotHandled-Exception`

Gets the reply as a primitive char.

`public long` **getLongReply()** `throws MessageException, NotHandled-Exception`

Gets the reply as a primitive long.

`public abstract boolean` **isAvailable()**

Checks whether a reply is available.

`public abstract void` **waitForReply(long duration)**

Waits for a reply until the specified period has elapsed.

`public abstract void` **waitForReply()**

Waits for a reply.

A.1.8 Class com.ibm.aglet.Message

public class **Message** implements Serializable

The Message class defines an object that holds its kind and arguments passed to the receiver.

A.1.8.1 Variables

public final static int **SYNCHRONOUS**

Indicates how a message was sent.

public final static int **FUTURE**

Indicates how a message was sent.

public final static int **ONEWAY**

Indicates how a message was sent.

public final static String **CLONE**

Used to prioritize system messages.

public final static String **DISPATCH**

Used to prioritize system messages.

public final static String **DISPOSE**

Used to prioritize system messages.

public final static String **DEACTIVATE**

Used to prioritize system messages.

public final static String **REVERT**

Used to prioritize system messages.

A.1.8.2 Constructors

public **Message(String kind)**

Constructs a message. The message object created by this constructor has a hash table that can be used for argument-value pairs.

public **Message(String kind, Object value)**

Constructs a message with an object argument value.

public **Message(String kind, int value)**

Constructs a message with an integer argument value.

public **Message(String kind, double value)**

Constructs a message with a double argument value.

public **Message(String kind, float value)**
Constructs a message with a float argument value.

public **Message(String kind, boolean value)**
Constructs a message with a Boolean argument value.

public **Message(String kind, char value)**
Constructs a message with a character argument value.

public **Message(String kind, long value)**
Constructs a message with a long argument value.

A.1.8.3 Methods

public String **getKind()**
Gets the kind of the message.

public boolean **sameKind(String kind)**
Checks whether the message is of the same kind as the specified string.

public boolean **sameKind(Message msg)**
Checks if the message is of the same kind as the specified message.

public long **getTimeStamp()**
Gets the time in milliseconds when the message was sent.

public Object **getArg()**
Gets the argument.

public int **getMessageType()**
Returns a type indicating how the message was sent.

public void **setArg(String name, Object value)**
Sets a value with an associated name.

public void **setArg(String name, boolean value)**
Sets a Boolean value with an associated name.

public void **setArg(String name, byte value)**
Sets a byte value with an associated name.

public void **setArg(String name, short value)**
Sets a short value with an associated name.

public void **setArg(String name, int value)**
Sets an int value with an associated name.

```
public void setArg(String name, double value)
```
Sets a double value with an associated name.

```
public void setArg(String name, float value)
```
Sets a float value with an associated name.

```
public void setArg(String name, char value)
```
Sets a character value with an associated name.

```
public void setArg(String name, long value)
```
Sets a long value with an associated name.

```
public Object getArg(String name)
```
Gets the value to which the specified key is mapped in this message.

```
public void sendReply(Object value)
```
Sends an object as reply.

```
public void sendReply()
```
Sends a reply without a specific value.

```
public void sendException(Exception ex)
```
Sends an exception as reply.

```
public void sendReply(int value)
```
Sends an integer as reply.

```
public void sendReply(double value)
```
Sends a double as reply.

```
public void sendReply(float value)
```
Sends a float as reply.

```
public void sendReply(boolean value)
```
Sends a Boolean as reply.

```
public void sendReply(char value)
```
Sends a character as reply.

```
public void sendReply(long value)
```
Sends a long as reply.

```
public void enableDeferedReply(boolean b)
```
Enables a deferred reply.

public boolean **equals(Object obj)**

Compares two Message objects.

A.1.9   Class com.ibm.aglet.ReplySet

public final class **ReplySet**

ReplySet is a container for FutureReply objects.

A.1.9.1 Constructors

public **ReplySet()**

Constructs a ReplySet object.

A.1.9.2 Methods

public synchronized boolean **hasMoreFutureReplies()**

Checks whether there are more FutureReply objects.

public boolean **isAnyAvailable()**

Checks whether there is any FutureReply object whose reply is available.

public boolean **areAllAvailable()**

Checks whether all FutureReply objects have received replies.

public int **countAvailable()**

Counts the number of available replies.

public int **countUnavailable()**

Counts the number of FutureReply objects that have no reply available.

public synchronized void **waitForNextFutureReply()**

Waits until the next reply is available or the specified period has elapsed.

public synchronized void **waitForNextFutureReply(long duration)**

Waits until the next reply is available.

public synchronized void **waitForAllReplies()**

Waits until all the replies are available.

public synchronized void **waitForAllReplies(long duration)**

Waits until all the replies are available or the specified period has elapsed.

public synchronized FutureReply **getNextFutureReply()**

Gets the next FutureReply object whose reply is available.

public synchronized void **addFutureReply(FutureReply reply)**
Adds the FutureReply object to this ReplySet.

A.1.10   Exception com.ibm.aglet.AgletException

public class **AgletException** extends Exception
Signals that an aglet exception has occurred.

A.1.10.1 Constructors

public **AgletException()**
Constructs an AgletException.

public **AgletException(String msg)**
Constructs an AgletException with the specified detail message.

A.1.11   Exception com.ibm.aglet.AgletNotFoundException

public class **AgletNotFoundException** extends AgletException
Signals that the aglet could not be found.

A.1.11.1 Constructors

public **AgletNotFoundException()**
Constructs an AgletNotFoundException.

public **AgletNotFoundException(String msg)**
Constructs an AgletNotFoundException with the specified detail message.

A.1.12   Exception com.ibm.aglet.InvalidAgletException

public class **InvalidAgletException** extends AgletException
Signals that the aglet proxy is not valid any longer.

A.1.12.1 Constructors

public **InvalidAgletException()**
Constructs an InvalidAgletException.

public **InvalidAgletException(String msg)**
Constructs an InvalidAgletException with the specified detail message.

A.1.13   Exception com.ibm.aglet.MessageException

public class **MessageException** extends AgletException
Signals that the exception occurred while processing the message.

A.1.13.1 Constructors

public **MessageException(Throwable ex)**
Constructs a MessageException.

public **MessageException(Throwable ex, String msg)**
Constructs a MessageException with the specified detail message.

A.1.13.2 Methods

public Throwable **getException()**
Gets the exception.

A.1.14   Exception com.ibm.aglet.NotHandledException

public class **NotHandledException** extends AgletException
Signals that a message was not handled by an aglet.

A.1.14.1 Constructors

public **NotHandledException()**
Constructs a NotHandledException.

public **NotHandledException(String msg)**
Constructs a NotHandledException with the specified detail message.

A.1.15   Exception com.ibm.aglet.RequestRefusedException

public class **RequestRefusedException** extends AgletException
Signals that a request was refused.

A.1.15.1 Constructors

public **RequestRefusedException()**
Constructs a RequestRefusedException.

public **RequestRefusedException(String msg)**
Constructs a RequestRefusedException with the specified detail message.

A.1.16   Exception com.ibm.aglet.ServerNotFoundException

public class **ServerNotFoundException** extends IOException
Signals that the server is not available.

A.1.16.1 Constructors

public **ServerNotFoundException()**
Constructs a ServerNotFoundException.

public **ServerNotFoundException(String msg)**
Constructs a ServerNotFoundException with the specified detail message.

A.2   com.ibm.aglet.event Package

A.2.1   Interface com.ibm.aglet.event.CloneListener

public interface **CloneListener** extends Serializable
The listener interface for receiving aglet clone events.

A.2.1.1 Methods

public abstract void **onCloning(CloneEvent event)**
Invoked when an aglet is being cloned.

public abstract void **onClone(CloneEvent event)**
Invoked after an aglet was cloned. This event is delivered only to the cloned aglet.

public abstract void **onCloned(CloneEvent event)**
Invoked after an aglet was cloned. This event is delivered only to the original aglet.

A.2.2   Interface com.ibm.aglet.event.MobilityListener

public interface **MobilityListener** extends Serializable
The listener interface for receiving aglet mobility events.

A.2.2.1 Methods

public abstract void **onDispatching(MobilityEvent event)**
Invoked when the aglet is being dispatched.

public abstract void **onReverting(MobilityEvent event)**
Invoked when the aglet is retracted.

public abstract void **onArrival(MobilityEvent event)**

Invoked just after an aglet has arrived at the destination.

A.2.3   Interface com.ibm.aglet.event.PersistencyListener

public interface **PersistencyListener** extends Serializable

The listener interface for receiving aglet persistency events.

A.2.3.1 Methods

public abstract void **onDeactivating(PersistencyEvent event)**

Invoked when an aglet is being deactivated.

Public abstract void **onActivation(PersistencyEvent event)**

Invoked just after the aglet is activated.

A.2.4   Class com.ibm.aglet.event.AgletEvent

public class **AgletEvent**

The top-level event of aglet events.

A.2.4.1 Constructor

Public **AgletEvent(Object source, int id)**

Constructs an AgletEvent with source and identity.

A.2.4.2 Methods

public int **getID()**

Gets the identity of this event.

A.2.5   Class com.ibm.aglet.event.AgletEventListener

public class **AgletEventListener** implements CloneListener, MobilityListener, PersistencyListener, Externalizable

The aglet event listener class is a container class for all listeners.

A.2.5.1 Constructors

Public **AgletEventListener(MobilityListener listener1, Mobility-Listener listener2)**

Constructs an AgletEventListener object with the specified two mobility listener objects.

public **AgletEventListener(CloneListener listener1, CloneListener listener2)**

Constructs an AgletEventListener object with the specified two clone listener objects.

Public **AgletEventListener(PersistencyListener listener1, PersistencyListener listener2)**

Constructs an AgletEventListener object with the specified two persistency listener objects.

A.2.5.2 Methods

public int **size()**

Returns the number of listeners.

public void **addCloneListener(CloneListener listener)**

Adds the specified clone listener.

public void **addMobilityListener(MobilityListener listener)**

Adds the specified mobility listener.

public void **addPersistencyListener(PersistencyListener listener)**

Adds the specified persistency listener.

public void **removeCloneListener(CloneListener listener)**

Removes the specified clone listener.

public void **removeMobilityListener(MobilityListener listener)**

Removes the specified mobility listener.

public void **removePersistencyListener(PersistencyListener listener)**

Removes the specified persistency listener.

public void **onCloning(CloneEvent event)**

Calls the onCloning methods in the listeners with the specified clone event.

public void **onClone(CloneEvent event)**

Calls the onClone methods in the listeners with the specified clone event.

public void **onCloned(CloneEvent event)**

Calls the onCloned methods in the listeners with the specified clone event.

public void **onDispatching(MobilityEvent event)**

Calls the onDispatching methods in the listeners with the specified mobility event.

public void **onReverting(MobilityEvent event)**

Calls the onReverting methods in the listeners with the specified mobility event.

public void **onArrival(MobilityEvent event)**

Calls the onArrival methods in the listeners with the specified mobility event.

public void **onDeactivating(PersistencyEvent event)**

Calls the onDeactivating methods in the listeners with the specified persistency event.

public void **onActivation(PersistencyEvent event)**

Calls the onActivation methods in the listeners with the specified persistency event.

A.2.6   Class com.ibm.aglet.event.CloneAdapter

public class **CloneAdapter** implements CloneListener

The adapter that receives clone events. This class is provided as a convenience to let you easily create listeners by extending this class and overriding only the methods of interest.

A.2.6.1 Constructor

public **CloneAdapter()**

Constructs the CloneAdapter object.

A.2.6.2 Methods

public void **onCloning(CloneEvent event)**

Initializes the cloned aglet.

public void **onClone(CloneEvent event)**

Initializes the cloned aglet.

public void **onCloned(CloneEvent event)**

Is called in the original aglet when the cloning has taken place.

A.2.7   Class com.ibm.aglet.event.CloneEvent

public class **CloneEvent** extends AgletEvent

The clone event occurs when the cloning of an aglet is attempted.

A.2.7.1 Variables

public final static int **AGLET_CLONE_FIRST**

Marks the first identity in the range of clone event identities.

public final static int **AGLET_CLONE_LAST**

Marks the last identity in the range of clone event identities.

public final static int **CLONING**
The CLONING event type.

public final static int **CLONE**
The CLONE event type.

public final static int **CLONED**
The CLONED event type.

A.2.7.2 Constructor

public **CloneEvent(int identity, AgletProxy aglet)**
Constructs the CloneEvent object with the specified identity and aglet.

A.2.7.3 Methods

public **AgletProxy getAgletProxy()**
Returns the aglet proxy that is the source of the event.

A.2.8 Class com.ibm.aglet.event.MobilityAdapter

public class **MobilityAdapter** implements MobilityListener
The adapter that receives mobility events. This class is provided as a convenience to let you easily create listeners by extending this class and overriding only the methods of interest.

A.2.8.1 Constructor

public **MobilityAdapter()**
Constructs the MobilityAdapter object.

A.2.8.2 Methods

public void **onDispatching(MobilityEvent event)**
Called when an attempt is made to dispatch the aglet.

public void **onArrival(MobilityEvent event)**
Initializes the newly arrived aglet.

public void **onReverting(MobilityEvent event)**
Called when someone from a remote location attempts to retract the aglet.

A.2.9   Class `com.ibm.aglet.event.MobilityEvent`

public class **MobilityEvent** extends AgletEvent
The mobility event occurs when the aglet is about to move.

A.2.9.1 Variables

public final static int **AGLET_MOBILITY_FIRST**
Marks the first identity in the range of mobility event identities.

public final static int **AGLET_MOBILITY_LAST**
Marks the last identity in the range of mobility event identities.

public final static int **DISPATCHING**
The DISPATCHING event type.

public final static int **REVERTING**
The REVERTING event type.

public final static int **ARRIVAL**
The ARRIVAL event type.

A.2.9.2 Constructor

public **MobilityEvent(int id, AgletProxy target, URL loc)**
Constructs a mobility event with specified identity, target, and location.

A.2.9.3 Methods

public AgletProxy **getAgletProxy()**
Returns the aglet proxy that is the source of the event.

public URL **getLocation()**
Gets the location.

A.2.10   Class `com.ibm.aglet.event.PersistencyAdapter`

public class **PersistencyAdapter** implements PersistencyListener
The adapter that receives persistency events. This class is provided as a convenience to let you easily create listeners by extending this class and overriding only the methods of interest.

A.2.10.1 Constructor

public **PersistencyAdapter()**
Constructs a PersistencyAdapter object.

A.2.10.2 Methods

public void **onDeactivating(PersistencyEvent event)**
Called when an attempt is made to deactivate the aglet.

public void **onActivation(PersistencyEvent event)**
Initializes the newly activated aglet.

A.2.11   Class com.ibm.aglet.event.PersistencyEvent

public class **PersistencyEvent** extends AgletEvent
The persistency event.

A.2.11.1 Variables

public final static int **AGLET_PERSISTENCY_FIRST**
Marks the first identity in the range of persistency event identities.

public final static int **AGLET_PERSISTENCY_LAST**
Marks the last identity in the range of persistency event identities.

public final static int **DEACTIVATING**
The DEACTIVATING event type.

public final static int **ACTIVATION**
The ACTIVATION event type.

A.2.11.2 Constructor

public **PersistencyEvent(int id, AgletProxy aglet, long duration)**
Constructs a PersistencyEvent with the specified identity, aglet proxy, and duration.

A.2.11.3 Methods

public AgletProxy **getAgletProxy()**
Returns the aglet proxy that is the source of the event.

public long **getDuration()**
Gets the duration.

Bibliography

We offer this list of works for further reading on related topics. The list is by no means exhaustive, and other excellent works exist on all of these topics.

Java and Object-Oriented Topics

java.sun.com, JavaSoft, Sun Microsystems, Inc.   The latest information on Java and related topics, including Java releases and online documentation.

K. Arnold and J. Gosling, *The Java Programming Language, Second edition*, Addison Wesley Longman, Reading, MA, 1998.

E. Gamma, R. Helm, R. Johnson, and J. Vlissides, *Design Patterns*, Addison Wesley Longman, Reading, MA, 1995.   The design pattern bible, this book contains excellent descriptions of common object-oriented design patterns.

A. Yonezawa and M. Tokoro, editors, *Object-Oriented Concurrent Programming*, The MIT Press, Cambridge, MA, 1987.

Security Topics

W. M. Farmer, J. D. Guttman, and V. Swrup, "Security for Mobile Agents: Issues and Requirements," in *Proceedings of the 19th National Information Systems Security Conference* (NISSC 96), 1996.

Li Gong, "Java Security Architecture (JDK1.2)," *JavaSoft*, July 1997.

J. J. Ordille, "When Agents Roam, Who Can You Trust?" in *Proceedings of the First Conference on Emerging Technologies and Applications in Communications*, May 1996.

J. Tardo and L. Valente, "Mobile Agent Security and Telescript," in *Proceedings of IEEE CompCon 96*, IEEE Computer Society Press, Los Alamitos, CA, 1996.

Agent Topics

S. Franklin and A. Graesser, "Is It an Agent, or Just a Program?: A Taxonomy for Autonomous Agents," in *Proceedings of the Third International Workshop on Agent Theories, Architectures, and Languages*, Springer-Verlag, 1996.

M. R. Genesereth and S. P. Ketchpel, "Software Agents," Communications of the ACM, 37(7):48–53, July 1994.

Y. Labrou and T. Finin, "A Proposal for a New KQML Specification," Technical Report CS-97-03, Computer Science and Electrical Engineering Department, University of Maryland Baltimore County, Baltimore, 1997. This report describes a modernized and improved version of KQML.

Mobile Agent Topics

Ara, *www.uni-kl.de/AG-Nehmer/Ara*.

D. Chess, B. Grosof, C. Harrison, D. Levine, C. Parris, and G. Tsudik, "Itinerant Agents for Mobile Computing," *IEEE Personal Communications Magazine*, 2(5):34–49, October 1995.

Dartmouth College, Agent Tcl, *www.cs.dartmouth.edu/~agent*.

General Magic Inc., Odyssey, *www.genmagic.com/agents*.

C. G. Harrison, D. M. Chess, and A. Kershenbaum, "Mobile Agents: Are They a Good Idea?" IBM Research Report, RC 19887, 1994.

J. Kiniry and D. Zimmerman, "A Hands-on Look at Mobile Java Agents," *IEEE Internet Computing*, 21–30, July–August, 1997.

Mitsubishi, Concordia, *www.meitca.com/HSL/Projects/Concordia*.

The Object Management Group, "The Mobile Agent System Interoperability Facility," OMG TC Document orbos/97-10-05, The Object Management Group, Framingham, MA, 1997. *www.omg.org/library/schedule/Technology_Adoptions.htm#Mobile_Agents_Facility*. The MASIF specification from OMG.

ObjectSpace Inc., Voyager, *www.objectspace.com/voyager*.

TACOMA, *www.cs.uit.no/DOS/Tacoma*.

J. White, "Mobile Agents," in *Software Agents*, J. Bradshaw, ed., MIT Press, Cambridge, MA, 1997. Seminal paper by the inventor of the mobile agent paradigm.

Aglet Topics

www.trl.ibm.co.jp/aglets, IBM Tokyo Research Laboratory, IBM Japan. The latest information on Aglets Workbench, including latest release, sample aglets, and online documentation. Updates to this book and examples from it are also available at *http://www.awl.com/cseng/titles/0-201-32582-9*.

Y. Aridor and D. B. Lange, "Agent Design Patterns: Elements of Agent Application Design," in *Proceedings of the Second International Conference on Autonomous Agents (Agents '98)*, ACM Press, New York, 1998.

G. Karjoth, D. B. Lange, and M. Oshima, "A Security Model for Aglets," *IEEE Internet Computing*, 1(4):68–77, 1997. This paper describes the first cut of a security model for Aglets.

D. B. Lange, M. Oshima, G. Karjoth, and K. Kosaka, "Aglets: Programming Mobile Agents in Java, " in *Proceedings of Worldwide Computing and Its Applications (WWCA'97), Lecture Notes in Computer Science, Vol. 1274*, Springer Verlag, New York, 1997.

D. B. Lange and Mitsuru Oshima, "Mobile Agents with Java: The Aglet API," *World Wide Web Journal*, Baltzer Science Publishers, Bussum, The Netherlands, 1998.

Y. Nakamura and G. Yamamoto, "An Electronic Marketplace Framework Based on Mobile Agents," Research Report, RT0224, IBM Research, Tokyo Research Laboratory, Japan, 1997. An interesting report that presents the experience gained from using Aglets on a real Internet application.

B. Sommers, "Agents: Not Just for Bond Anymore," *JavaWorld*, *www.javaworld.com/javaworld/jw-04-1997/jw-04-agents.html*.

B. Venners, "Under the Hood: The Architecture of Aglets," *JavaWorld*, *www.javaworld.com/javaworld/jw-04-1997/jw-04-hood.html*.

B. Venners, "Solve Real Problems with Aglets, a Type of Mobile Agent," *JavaWorld*, *www.javaworld.com/javaworld/jw-05-1997/jw-05-hood.html*.

Index